Distance Counseling:

Expanding the Counselor's Reach and Impact

Editors

James F. Malone
Randy M. Miller
Garry R. Walz

Counseling Outfitters, LLC

in association with

ReadyMinds, LLC

AMERICAN COUNSELING
ASSOCIATION

Distance Counseling: Expanding the Counselor's Reach and Impact

10 9 8 7 6 5 4 3 2 1

Counseling Outfitters, LLC
P.O. Box 1208
Ann Arbor, MI 48106-1208

Cover photograph by Garry R. Walz, Ph.D.
Cover design by Kaye Davis, Greensboro, NC and TCA Graphics, Naples, FL
Editing and production supervision by Jeanne C. Bleuer, Ph.D.

The photograph was personally produced by me and represented the unanimous choice of the editors. It is intended to convey the essentially limitless outreach of Distance Counseling. The reflection of the sun on the water portrays the birth of a new day and new perspectives that can be brought about through Distance Counseling. We believe that, appropriately used, Distance Counseling can brighten the days of those fortunate to experience it.

Garry R. Walz, Editor-In-Chief

Library of Congress Cataloging in Publication Data
Malone, James.

Distance counseling/James Malone, Randy Miller, & Garry Walz
      p.cm.

Includes bibliographical references

ISBN 13: 978-0-9795668-0-6 (alk. Paper)

Table of Contents

Preface. . . . . *iii*
About the Editors . . . . *v*
About the Authors . . . . *vii*

Chapter One 1
More Than an Introduction
Garry R. Walz

Chapter Two 9
Understanding Distance Counseling
James F. Malone

Chapter Three 37
The Distance Credentialed Counselor
Susan P. Shafer and Thomas W. Clawson

Chapter Four 43
Who Can Perform Distance Counseling?
DeeAnna Merz Nagel

Chapter Five 53
The Assessment Process via Distance Counseling
Jill Lumsden

Chapter Six 65
**How to Organize and Launch a Distance Counseling
Program**
Michelle Relyea

Chapter Seven 75
**A Step-by-Step Approach for Adopting and Using
Distance Counseling As a Private Practitioner**
Denise E. Saunders

Contents

Chapter Eight 91
Distance Counseling in Action
Karen Ricci

Chapter Nine. 107
**The University College London (UCL)/ReadyMinds
Career Counseling Program: An International
Distance Counseling Partnership**
Marco Federighi

Chapter Ten. 119
**Challenges and Special Problems in Distance
Counseling: How to Respond to Them**
Heidi B. Ravis

Chapter Eleven 133
**Ethical Guidelines, Legal and Regulatory Issues
in Distance Counseling**
James F. Malone

Chapter Twelve 149
Ensuring the Quality of Distance Counseling
Edwin Schwartz

Appendix A: 159
**The Use of Telephone Help Lines in Career
Information and Guidance**
A.G. Watts & Gareth Dent

Appendix B: Epilogue 181
**The ReadyMinds Story: Transforming a Vision
into a Reality ... and What Comes Next?**
Randy M. Miller

Preface

To comprehensively address the wide range of tasks involved in implementing Distance Counseling, the editors recruited ten authors to assist in the writing of the chapters for this book. Each chapter author has demonstrated a high level of skill in the area of Distance Counseling relevant to his/her chapter. The editors saw this as the most effective way to share with the reader the most up-to-date insights on how to perform Distance Counseling. The result is that, in addition to the collective knowledge and experience of the three editors, a large number of other writers have contributed their insights on specific important aspects of Distance Counseling.

Two unique contributions have also been included as Appendix A and Appendix B. In Appendix A, "The Use of Telephone Helplines in Career Information and Guidance," Tony Watts and Gareth Dent share their thoughts and experiences in implementing and managing a telephone helpline, Learndirect, in the United Kingdom. It is always interesting and useful to have the perspective of how a new counseling initiative is implemented in another country. Though very different in goals and implementation, Learndirect involves many of the same principles, skills, and issues relevant to the Distance Counseling model presented in this book.

In Appendix B, "The ReadyMinds Story: Transforming a Vision into a Reality...and What Comes Next?" Randy Miller presents an engaging narrative of how and why he created ReadyMinds and the struggles involved in forming the successful company it is today. Based on his own experiences as a college student, he saw the need for a new way to deliver career counseling so as to expand the reach of the career counselors. This, combined with his entrepreneurial spirit, led to his creating a company that offers high quality training for counselors who wish to become Distance Counselors or to incorporate Distance Counseling skills into their own traditional counseling practice. While many training programs have emerged in recent years, the ReadyMinds program is distinguished by its intensive training by highly experienced Distance Counseling specialists

and its commitment to helping trainees meet CCE standards for Distance
Credentialed Counselor certification.

As editors, we wanted to produce a volume that, taken overall, was like a
symphony in which different members of the orchestra contributed their
own expertise to the total production – sometimes playing together and
other times offering solos. In any case, it was our intent to provide as
comprehensive coverage of Distance Counseling as possible so that each
reader can draw from it what they need and want to learn. It is up to you,
the reader, to determine how successful we were. We welcome hearing your
reactions and recommendations. Hopefully, this book will stimulate you to
incorporate Distance Counseling into some aspect of your helping services.

Pleasant reading!

Garry R. Walz, Ph.D., NCC
Editor-In-Chief
GRWalz@aol.com

About the Editors

James F. Malone, Ph.D., is the Director of Counseling, Training & Supervision for ReadyMinds. A graduate counselor educator and career development practitioner in schools, universities and the private sector for 35 years, Dr. Malone has applied his wide professional experience to the research and development of ReadyMinds Distance Counseling and Training Programs since 1998. Over the last several years he has read and evaluated the comprehensive entry questionnaires for thousands of ReadyMinds clients from a wide variety of educational, occupational and organizational environments. Each registered client receives a careful analysis of counseling needs and validated online assessment prior to being assigned to an appropriately matched ReadyMinds Career Counselor.

Based on his consistent, in-depth work with Distance Counseling clients and their dynamic needs, Dr. Malone has become intimately familiar with the effective practices that this evolving specialty promises to bring to the counseling profession. He has also developed Distance based protocols to oversee the practice and supervision of ReadyMinds Case Managers and Counselors throughout various locations across the United States.
Dr. Malone has presented and published frequently while managing various ReadyMinds Distance Counseling services including the Distance Credentialed Counselor (DCC) Training Program. Dr. Malone holds Fellow membership status in the National Career Development Association and is a Licensed Mental Health Counselor in New York State with certifications as a National Certified Counselor, Distance Credentialed Counselor and an Approved Clinical Supervisor.

Randy M. Miller, B.S., is CEO of Ready Minds, LLC., which he founded in 1997 to help individuals improve the way they think about their personal and career growth. He spent five years studying the industry, financing proprietary research, and recruiting experts in career counseling, education, business, and human resources in order to create a first class counseling service. He currently oversees corporate strategy and business development to expand relationships with educational, government, and corporate partners.

Throughout his career, Randy has sought to share his knowledge and experiences with others. He has served as a mentor, co-author, and motivational speaker, helping individuals gain a better understanding of themselves and their career interests. He has co-authored numerous publications, been featured on ABC's National Television Series *Business Week - Money Talks*; been interviewed and quoted by *MonsterTrak*, *MSN Encarta*, *Newsweek*, and *Kiplinger's Magazine*; and was recently featured in the National Career Development Association's *Starting and Growing a Business in the Global Marketplace: Career Entrepreneurs Share Stories and Strategies*.

Prior to founding ReadyMinds, Randy was vice president of a privately held, multi-million dollar New York manufacturing company that he helped co-found in 1989. He graduated from the University of Rhode Island's College of Business Administration where, from 1986-1988, he served as vice president of sales & marketing for Campus Connection, a national collegiate publication firm.

Garry R. Walz, Ph.D., NCC, established and directed the ERIC Counseling and Student Services Clearinghouse at the University of North Carolina at Greensboro. He started the clearinghouse at the University of Michigan in 1966 and served as its director until 1993, when it moved to North Carolina. He also served as Chair of the Counselor Education Department at the University of Michigan and is currently a University of Michigan Professor Emeritus.

Dr. Walz has authored and co-authored numerous books and articles and initiated and directed the award-winning ERIC/CASS *Virtual Libraries*. He has been a pioneer in training counselors in the use of technology, beginning with the design and implementation of annual training conferences in the early '80s. He is also co-editor of two books on Cybercounseling and Cyberlearning, published collaboratively by ERIC/CASS and the American Counseling Association.

Dr. Walz is a past president of the American Counseling Association, a past president of the Association for Counselor Education and Supervision, and a past chair of the Counseling and Human Development Foundation. In 2006, was named an ACA Fellow. His numerous professional awards include the ACA Gilbert and Kathleen Wrenn Humanitarian Award and the National Career Development Association's Eminent Professional Career Award. Dr. Walz was honored at a special 100 year anniversary ceremony as one of the 100 most distinguished alumni of the University of Minnesota's College of Education and Human Development.

About the Authors

Thomas W. Clawson, Ed.D., NCC, is the President and CEO of the National Board for Certified Counselors (NBCC) and its affiliates, the Center for Credentialing and Education (CCE) and the NBCC Foundation, located in Greensboro, North Carolina. He is a past president of the National Organization for Competency Assurance (NOCA) and a past Chairman of the National Commission for Certifying Agencies. The 350 member boards of NOCA certify over ten million professionals in the U.S. and Canada.

Marco Federighi graduated in physics from the University of Pisa (Italy) in 1980 and is now the Sub-Dean of Engineering at UCL (London). He has worked as a research scientist with GEC and Marconi, and later at UCL, in the fields of optoelectronics and of optical telecommunications. He is now responsible for the development of teaching programs, particularly international collaborative programs, in the Faculty of Engineering Sciences at UCL.

Jill A. Lumsden, Ed.S., NCC, DCC, is the Project Manager of the online Career Portfolio at Florida State University. She is also a counselor and trainer for ReadyMinds. She is co-author of several articles and book chapters related to eportfolios, technology in counseling, and online assessment. She holds certifications as a National Certified Counselor and Distance Credentialed Counselor.

DeeAnna Merz Nagel, M.Ed., LPC, DCC, is CEO and President of Merz Consulting, Inc., an organization that provides a variety of counseling, assessment and consultation services. She serves as a trainer for ReadyMinds and is a past president of the International Society for Mental Health Online (ISMHO). She holds licenses in New Jersey and Georgia and several certifications including Approved Clinical Supervisor, Certified Rehabilitation Counselor, and Distance Credentialed Counselor.

Heidi B. Ravis, EdM, NCC, DCC, is a counselor, case manager and trainer for ReadyMinds. She also serves as a Distance Counselor for Graduate Students and Alumni in the Office of Career Services at Long

Island University, Brooklyn, NY, in a partnership with ReadyMinds. She is co-author of CEU Courses and the Distance Credential Counselor Training Program, and serves as a Lead Trainer for ReadyMinds. She has worked in a range of educational, community and not-for-profit settings, and has special expertise in clinical career counseling. She holds certifications as a National Certified Counselor and Distance Credentialed Counselor.

Michelle Relyea, MSEd, NCC, DCC, is the Dean of Academic and Instructional Resources at Long Island University in Brooklyn, New York, with responsibility for Career Services, Academic Advisement, First-Year Experience Programs, and various grant initiatives. Prior to her appointment to Dean, she was the Director of Career Services and Cooperative Education for four years as well as a Career Counselor for three years at LIU. In addition to her administrative responsibilities, she teaches a variety of courses and has re-designed the Career Readiness Course at LIU. Michelle is a counselor, case manager, trainer, and assists with business development for ReadyMinds. Michelle holds certification as a National Certified Counselor and Distance Credentialed Counselor.

Karen L. Ricci, MA, NCC, DCC, serves as College/Career Counselor at Fallbrook Union High School, Fallbrook, CA, and is also a counselor with ReadyMinds. She has worked in a variety of educational settings and has a special expertise in working with clients with diverse backgrounds, namely, military individuals, teens and re-entry or career changing women. She is involved in grant proposals related to technology efforts within the academic sector. She holds certifications as a National Certified Counselor and Distance Credentialed Counselor.

Denise E. Saunders, Ph.D., NCC, DCC, is a counselor and trainer for ReadyMinds. She also maintains a private practice in Chapel Hill, North Carolina providing mental health and career counseling and consultation services to her clients. She has worked in higher education with expertise in student counseling, college career services and teaching and instruction. Her research interests have focused on the connections between career and mental health counseling. She has co-authored several publications related to this topic including the *Career Thoughts Inventory*, a career counseling assessment tool. She is a Licensed Psychologist in the state of North Carolina, a National Certified Counselor, and a Distanced Credentialed Counselor.

Edwin S. Schwartz, MA, is the Vice President of Operations for ReadyMinds. Mr. Schwartz has an extensive background that includes working on college campuses, as well holding key management positions within the business sector. At ReadyMinds, Mr. Schwartz oversees the counseling and training areas and coordinates the objectives of the ReadyMinds Counseling and Training Programs with the overall business goals of the company.

Susan P. Shafer, M.Ed., is the Executive Projects Director for the National Board for Certified Counselors and its affiliates. With a background in mental health counseling, Ms. Shafer has been involved in the certification development of professionals in the United States and around the world for the past ten years. Ms. Shafer has lectured around the world on the importance of developing strong standards of practice, and enforcing clear ethical codes of conduct through quality credentialing.

Appendix A Authors

Tony Watts, MA, MPhil, Hon DUniv, OBE, is a Founding Fellow of the National Institute for Careers Education and Counselling and Visiting Professor at the University of Derby and Canterbury Christ Church University. He was formerly Director of NICEC. His recent work has been particularly concerned with international policy issues related to career guidance and career development.

Gareth Dent, BA, is Director of Advice Services at Learndirect and has overseen the telephone service's development from the beginning. He was formerly Head of Adult Guidance Policy at the Department for Education and Employment in the UK.

CHAPTER ONE

More Than an Introduction

Garry R. Walz

I recently attended a college football game among a group of highly exuberant and supportive young fans. Their involvement in the game was typical; but, in one sense, it was very different from any game I had previously attended. What struck me was how much these young people used their cell phones with picture and text messaging to interact on what was happening - both with one another at the game and with friends away from the game. Internet chats were going on all around me, greatly expanding the focus of the game from the playing field to a plethora of interactions both within the immediate space of the stadium as well as around the country – and, most likely, around the world.

It was a dramatic illustration of how technology mediates how we relate and communicate. For me, as a counseling professional, it sharpened the message that clients who enter a counseling office today just aren't who they used to be! They're different on a number of dimensions; but, most significantly, they're used to relating and communicating with the aid of technology to a far greater degree than ever before. The challenge for us, as counselors, is: How do we respond and counsel this new breed of client?

This book goes a long way in providing insights as to how we might answer that question. Although it includes an interesting and useful discussion of the background of Distance Counseling and its theoretical underpinnings, it is basically a nuts and bolts approach to how counselors can apply and utilize Distance Counseling principles and tools. Through numerous personal "testimonials" by front-line experts in the Distance Counseling field, readers can learn how to effectively implement Distance Counseling practices as well as how to address potential challenges. It is unabashedly a "how-to" book that we present without apology because we believe unreservedly that ALL counselors can benefit from the use of Distance

Counseling in their work – whether they be private practitioners, agency or educational institution counselors, counselor educators, or non-degreed coach/helpers.

Like physical exercise, Distance Counseling functions most effectively if the user understands its strengths and limitations and applies it judiciously. It is probably appropriate to say that the power in the medium is not in using it or not using it, but in being able to customize it to meet the specific needs and interest of each client. Its utility for any given individual will vary greatly with how appropriate it is for use with that client. Much as exercise can be overdone or inappropriate outcomes expected, the right focus and goals are key to how successful the use of Distance Counseling will be.

What follows in this introduction are a few observations that may prove useful to persons developing their own personal belief system regarding the use of Distance Counseling. Clearly, the best practitioners of Distance Counseling are those who have thoughtfully considered how it augments their existing beliefs and counseling practices.

1) Adopting Something You Can Believe In

Critics of Distance Counseling, many of whom are jealous of its popularity, are prone to say that it lacks "solid research evidence" that it works. There is some truth to this in that, for all types of counseling, it is very difficult to apply rigorous experimental controls in evaluation studies. Still, a body of evidence does exist supporting the efficacy of counseling (see, for example, Sexton, Whiston, Bleuer, & Walz, 1997). Large numbers of practitioners as well as clients are supportive of it – frequently enthusiastically so. Distance Counseling, being still in the formative stages, is too new to have acquired a large body of research support; but, as detailed in Chapter Two, research support does exist and is growing. You can adopt and use Distance Counseling knowing that there is reasonable enough evidence (both quantitative and qualitative) for experimenting with it to see if it works for you. Until a larger body of evidence is amassed, a useful guide is: Does it work for you - do your clients achieve their goals and desired outcomes with the degree of certainty and regularity that you desire? Don't take someone else's word. Find out for yourself if it fits your style and needs. As you apply Distance Counseling tools, listen with your "third ear" to determine if you are achieving what you want and need. Be your own researcher as you practice Distance Counseling and become more proficient in its use. Much of what is taught in Distance Counseling training has been acquired just that way – trial with careful review – and selection based on the observed outcomes.

2) Being a " Go To" Counselor

I recently overheard a young student say to another young friend, "Can you believe there was a time when you had to dial up on a phone line to get an Internet connection?" Whereupon the friend said, "Really?? How could you ever do anything?" The conversation went on and concluded that if you couldn't get "right on" (i.e., with a high speed, preferably wireless, connection), you were definitely still in the Dark Ages.

However appropriate – or inappropriate – it may be, people are judged by others by the extent to which they opt for and use new technologies. This orientation is probably particularly potent among younger clients. To some extent, it is a phenomenon not unlike the mantra of an earlier generation – "You can't trust anyone over 30." The counselor who has adopted and uses new technologies is seen as more relevant and more understanding, thus a "Go to" counselor.

Acquiring a "Go to" image and being seen as "cool" can well work to insure a flow of youthful clients. Using Distance Counseling can certainly help a counselor connect with persons who, by definition, would not be seen going to the counseling office or having sessions with a shrink.

3) Promoting a Technologically Savvy Professional Image

It has been said that, of all the helping and artistic professions, counseling is among the greatest holdouts to the infusion of new technologies. Health professionals, musicians, even artists are seen as being more receptive to technology than are counselors. To a person struggling to cope with the demands of a technologically-driven age, a profession so resistive of technology to deliver its messages and/or offer services may well be judged as irrelevant, hopelessly out of touch, and old-fashioned. In some cases, that may just be true.

A counselor who has not seen the advantages that can accrue to his/her counseling by the plethora of technologies available may well not be able to help a person explore appropriate life/career choices. A person who is more at home with cell phones, Web sites, and I-Pods may find relating to someone who shuns such devices as being unable to be helpful to them.

Though it may border on the ridiculous to seemingly posit a "technology index" as a partial criterion for counseling effectiveness, the counselor who would score low on such an index not only misses out on the many advantages the use of new technology can bring to his/her services, but also runs the risk of being seen as out of step with the world as it is. The use of technology inherent in Distance Counseling works to communicate to potential clients that this counselor does utilize new innovations that can enhance their effectiveness.

Doesn't such a judgment affect your choice of a person whom you would go to for help or advice? I expect many of us would agree that it does.

4) Incorporating Distance Counseling as a Supplementary and Complementary Component of Traditional Counseling

When one considers the extent and range of the need for counseling, especially career counseling, in today's world, it seems both a practical and a moral imperative that all counselors acquire a modicum of competence in Distance Counseling. In so many ways, traditional counseling can be enhanced through the use of components of Distance Counseling without embracing Distance Counseling as a distinct and separate form of counseling.

> *Easing counselor/client contact*
> *Communicating between face-to-face sessions*
> *Providing a "hotline" for topics of immediate criticality*
> *Reaching clients who are geographically distant*
> *Expanding the availability of services to clients with limited means*

For all of these reasons and many more, it behooves counselors to augment their armamentarium of counseling tools with Distance Counseling interventions. Counselors who use Distance Counseling tools are clearly helping their clients by delivering a more potent counseling intervention. But they are equally benefiting themselves by expanding the number and quality of resources they can bring to their counseling practice.

Perhaps most of all, there does seem to be a moral imperative to the use of Distance Counseling. In a time of great need brought on by natural and man-made disasters such as Katrina and 9/11, the need for counseling far exceeds what we can provide through existing traditional delivery systems. Are we to turn our backs on those unfortunate people who, because of cost, geography, or circumstance, can not go to a counselor? It seems that now, more than ever before, the counseling profession should utilize all available means to assist people with their life choices. To remain a profession where people must present themselves to us is to deny the needs of many and to tarnish our image of a helping, caring profession.

5) Enhancing the Power of the User

It is rather common practice when viewing an innovation to pair it off against an existing resource, e.g., group counseling as contrasted with individual counseling. Typically, the emphasis in such comparisons is to think of the innovative practice as a discrete, separate practice that is being examined as a stand alone entity and to determine how it stacks up against current resources and practices. Such an approach is helpful in examining what are the characteristics of the new practice. But it lacks the focus on how the innovative approach will fit into and benefit existing practices.

It is perhaps more helpful to think of Distance Counseling not so much as a unique, separate entity, but rather as a new resource that not only brings its own unique contributions, but, more importantly, creates a powerful synergy among counseling resources and tools. By fusing Distance Counseling techniques with traditional counseling skills and resources, the mutual reinforcement can provide a power for bringing about desired outcomes far greater than could be achieved by either alone.

6) Increasing Technological Utilization with Limited Discarding of Conventional Approaches

Over the past several decades, we have witnessed the introduction of new technologies that have been broadly heralded as bringing forth major changes in public behavior. Videotapes were expected to eclipse movie theaters; and computers and the Internet were to bring forth a "paperless" workplace. Neither expectation has proved to be true. What did happen was that the new technology has been adopted and used, but the older technology also continues to be used. The two exist side by side with some mutual support between the two. In some cases, movies have actually stimulated video sales. The Internet did come into its own, but printed materials and certainly books are still often preferable to staring at a monitor for long periods of time.

My point is that Distance Counseling will not replace or even diminish conventional counseling. The two can co-exist with the special advantages of each. In certain circumstances, the advantages of Distance Counseling will diminish the use of face-to-face counseling. However, Distance Counseling will not curtail the use of the face-to-face counseling in situations where the latter is clearly superior.

I believe that counselors will need to strike a balance for relative emphasis in each counselor/client relationship. What is clear is that contemporary complete counselors (CCCs) use a myriad of counseling resources and continually update themselves in the use of those resources. For most counselors, this means that they will need to "get up to speed" to develop competence in Distance Counseling so that it can be used when circumstances call for its use. Lack of skill in Distance Counseling should not determine its use.

Like so many aspects of contemporary life, the capacity of counselors to be open to change and to adopt or adapt new technologies is key to their being able to adequately respond to the changing client base and the new concerns that clients bring to counseling. CCCs are not all things to all people, but are always striving to educate themselves in the use of new tools and strategies to maximize assistance to clients.

The Specifics of this Book

Even a quick perusal of this book will reveal several major characteristics. They are:

1) It focuses on career counseling, not on generic or mental health counseling.
2) It relies heavily on one of the oldest, most frequently used and reliable forms of technology – the telephone.

3) It describes a systemic Distance Counseling program that incorporates the use of: individual phone counseling; test taking; judicious use of the Internet; at-home review and reflection by the client between telephone interviews; the use of experienced, certified, and supervised counselors; and regular review and evaluation of program components.

4) It essentially presents the knowledge and insights gained through several years of experience of the ReadyMinds program, buttressed by reference to the developing research and experiential counseling literature.

5) It has a strong practical "you can use this now" orientation that can be incorporated into a formal training program or used in an individual self study approach.

As the founder and long-time director of ERIC/CASS, I chose to focus on this single program because it was the best example I know of that is an operating program of some continuing duration. Its operation has met one major criterion – success in the marketplace. There may well be others as good or better, but I am not aware of them. My motivation in initiating and seeing this book through to its being published was to give counselors a concise picture of how a conceptually sound and well-managed Distance Counseling program operates.

I believe the ideas and practices presented in this book extend to many settings and populations. Counselors can pick and choose ideas and practices they see as worthy to be added to their repertoire of counseling resources. The book also offers a complete program which, with further study and practice, can be adopted and implemented in many situations. At a minimum, I hope it will stimulate thought and discussion on which of the Distance Counseling practices should be adopted and how best to do so. I don't say "whether" because I believe we are past the point of that. We should utilize much or all of what Distance Counseling offers. But, of course, each counselor must determine for him/herself how much to adopt and incorporate into his/her own counseling practices. Hopefully, this book will aid counselors in the process of doing so.

CHAPTER TWO

Understanding Distance Counseling

James F. Malone

This chapter presents a detailed definition of Distance Counseling in operation and a comprehensive classification of discrete Distance Counseling services. Distance Counseling competencies are introduced; and an in-depth training program designed to assist counselors, coaches, and other helping professionals to work within their scope of practice is described. This training helps individuals master the skills necessary to adapt proven face-to-face counseling techniques to distance delivery modalities. A review of the current state of research with respect to the effectiveness of Distance Counseling is presented, followed by an examination of how the results of the research can inform this evolving specialty. Examples of specific programs and services are described. The chapter ends with a discussion of the importance of basing counseling practices on evidence and theory.

The following scenario depicts the actual adaptation of traditional face-to-face career-educational counseling to a technology-supported distance delivery model. The names of the counselor and school have been changed.

Dr. Jack Walsh had been providing excellent career and educational planning services to the Winston School of New Rochelle for several years. As a consultant to the students and parents, he was accustomed to meeting them during the junior year for a comprehensive evening meeting in which all of the important details of college planning were addressed. Jack would then schedule individual, one-hour face-to-face meetings with each family during the following week. At various points, he made follow-up visits to the campus throughout the remainder of the students' junior year and continued his visits when they were seniors. He assisted them with the details of their college planning, a task that included appropriate help with completing applications as well as sculpting a strategically sound final list of schools. On occasion, students and parents sent e-mails requesting specific information or contacted him by phone for more detailed discussion. The schools' administration, students, parents, and Jack himself were all quite satisfied with the process and outcomes of the program.

Approximately four years ago an unexpected event came about rather suddenly towards the end of the school year. It threatened to end Jack's involvement with the Winston School community. Family plans necessitated a move for Jack, a move that would bring him several hundred miles from the New Rochelle area. Rather than simply terminating the successful program, however, some creative problem solving led to its continuation; and in some ways, it even provided an enhancement.

As a counselor educator, Jack had been previously involved with research and training in developing Distance Counseling programs. He was thoroughly versed in both the challenges and opportunities that the distance delivery of counseling services involved. What better application could this evolving specialty enjoy than in this situation? After careful consideration and discussion with school administrators and a student-parent group, Jack decided to design a new college counseling program that would take advantage of distance-delivered counseling communications that expand the reach of face-to-face services through e-mail and telephone counseling services.

Jack now drives down to the school at key planning points during the fall and spring semesters. He spends time establishing an initial relationship with his students and parents during the spring of their junior year, and he visits again in the fall of their senior year. However, in between these face-to-face contacts, there is a continuous flow of communication via Distance Counseling services.

Certain strategic planning had to take place in order to explain, establish, and maintain the program. During the junior year meeting, Jack spelled out the details of the Distance Counseling program enhancements including rationale, ethical guidelines, and supporting research about technology-assisted counseling services. Students and parents received information regarding encryption, Internet security, response time-frame expectations, and other important logistical issues that surround the joining of technology with counseling. Over the last four years there has been widespread acceptance and use of these distance services. Students, staff, and parents are able to receive detailed answers to their inquiries very quickly–usually within 24-48 hours. Thoughtful and insightful consideration is always exercised by Jack with respect to whether "between-the-lines" messages within an e-mail deserve a follow-up phone call.

Letters of recommendation are sent via an encrypted Web-based e-mail service that is also available to students. In short, Jack and his clients are convinced that this model is in some ways actually superior to the services he was accustomed to offering as part of a public high school guidance staff for most of his career. Parents and students enjoy the convenience, efficiency, and effectiveness of this service.

Why Engage in Distance Counseling?

Individuals familiar with school counseling can easily grasp the value of distance enhanced counseling contacts with students and parents. Instead of parents taking time off from work to meet with the counselor, they can send inquiries and receive information via e-mail or make telecounseling appointments. In many cases, answers to questions can be provided with greater efficiency than in situations where waiting several days for an appointment may be the alternative. In fact, there are school districts and colleges who have already moved to establishing secure, encrypted e-mail and chat platforms. This technology allows faculty, parents, students, and administrative staff to communicate regarding topics that range from attendance and prospective college admissions decisions to homework assignments and academic progress.

Other similar scenarios are easy to imagine. Picture, for example, a corporate coach who has clients in a distant city or clients whose work schedules render in-person visits quite inconvenient. Think of career services counselors on a college campus who may reach the shy or reluctant student who prefers the privacy of meeting virtually rather than in person. Imagine the student who would like to forward a draft copy of a job search cover letter for the counselor's critique, with subsequent options for a face-to-face meeting, chat session, or a telephone appointment. Most of our current students have grown up with e-mail and Instant Messaging. Many of them really *prefer* electronic communication with a counselor. They find it more efficient and convenient. For some individuals, writing may be a more self-expressive way of seeking assistance, and communicating online feels less restrictive and inhibiting (Suler, 2004b). Imagine the efficiency of forwarding a working copy of a resume to the coach or counselor who can then use appropriate technology to offer a critique and e-mail the document back with notes and suggestions. What about the thousands of distance learners who have every right to the same availability and level of student services that on-campus students enjoy? Finally, consider the fact that alumni are most likely spread all over the country or even abroad. A visit to the career services office on campus is simply out of the question, but distance services can provide valuable career planning assistance.

The example of Dr. Jack Walsh and the related scenarios cited above reflect examples of the practical convenience that Distance Counseling can provide. However, we also have to consider many additional factors that surround technology-supported counseling, such as effectiveness of the service, informed consent, ethical guidelines, privacy and confidentiality, and educating the client with respect to the entire Distance Counseling process. Clearly, there are also possible complications that the counselor and client may encounter. Potential problems are well known: the lack of visual cues, possible misunderstandings, security breaches and threats to confidentiality, particularly fragile clients, or clients whose technical or communication skills render them poor candidates for this type of counseling. We acknowledge and appreciate the potential challenges here. We believe that, in most cases, strategic and appropriate planning, which includes careful client screening, can surmount many of these difficulties.

Since the term "Distance Counseling" may invite various interpretations, a description of well-designed and effective Distance Counseling is needed at this early juncture. Indeed, the literature refers frequently to Online Counseling, Cybercounseling, Webcounseling, and Technology-Assisted Counseling. For example, Bloom and Walz (2000, 2004) have published two comprehensive treatments under the rubric of *cybercounseling and cyberlearning* to describe the work of counselors and educational professionals who have embraced the challenge of harnessing the power of technology and the Internet as a unique way of offering helping services.

At ReadyMinds, we prefer to use the more generic name, Distance Counseling, because it encompasses the many intervention strategies that electronic communication and technology afford. The following definition is the one ReadyMinds uses in its own proprietary career counseling and planning work as well as in its Distance Credentialed Counselor (DCC) Training Program (Malone, Miller, & Ravis, 2003). Much of this chapter and, in fact, the remaining chapters of this book will seek to amplify and explain the carefully chosen language that comprises this definition.

> *Distance Counseling is an evolving specialty that consists of carefully designed helping services, provided by appropriately trained and experienced counseling professionals. Distance Counselors employ the thoughtful use of technologies (synchronous, asynchronous, and computerized counseling programs) in order to assist clients to function with, or grow towards, increased wellness in their personal and professional lives.*
>
> *With eyes consistently focused on building and maintaining the working alliance, Distance Counselors seek to adapt effective, evidence-based counseling practices from face-to-face models by delivering them with similarly positive outcomes via electronic means that are deemed suitable to their clients' needs. At the same time, Distance Counselors also help their clients by exploiting the many promising benefits and advantages that initial research suggests are unique to technology.* (p. 27)

A Clear Understanding of Distance Counseling

A clear understanding of various Distance Counseling modalities is essential so that counselors may discuss the advantages, disadvantages, challenges, and unique benefits of such services with clients as well as with colleagues. When addressing the assessment and contracting phases of telecounseling, Rosenfeld (1997) cites the client's need for concrete information and understanding of services in the interest of ensuring informed consent. In addition, schools, institutions, and corporations wishing to offer Distance Counseling or coaching will certainly need to promote internal discussions among counselors, technology staff, and administrative personnel so that all parties involved are professionally united with respect to their responsibilities in providing these services.

Financial investments in training and professional staff development will ultimately flow from a grounded belief that distance services will benefit all constituencies involved.

One of the clearest presentations of the various faces Distance Counseling can assume is found in the document entitled *The Practice of Internet Counseling* on the Web site of the National Board for Certified Counselors (2001). *The Taxonomy for Defining Face-to Face and Technology-Assisted Distance Counseling* (http://www.nbcc.org/webethics2) describes the special characteristics of synchronous delivery formats (in real time with little or no delay in communication between counselor and client) such as telecounseling, chat, or video-supported models. It also presents asynchronous models including e-mail counseling and message board communication strategies that allow time between the sending and receiving of text.

While the *Taxonomy* does not address the topic specifically, Distance Counseling also provides clients access to a variety of computerized counseling programs that may be used either with or without direct involvement of the counselor. Our professional bias leans very much towards built-in counselor contact with clients who engage in computerized programs, especially in cases where there is suspicion that the individual may be experiencing a significant degree of conflict, anxiety, or other emotional distress.

The remainder of the *Taxonomy* document outlines the 14 standards that govern the ethical practice of Internet Counseling. Several additional professional counselor associations have published their own guidelines and ethical standards that govern the delivery of online counseling and related services. We will deal with these important ethical issues as well as related legal/regulatory questions in Chapter Eleven.

How Research Informs Practice in Distance Counseling

Several questions face counselors or coaches who are considering the option of offering distance services. Will their work supplement face-to-face client contact or will it stand alone? What is their scope of practice? What is their work setting, and what kinds of challenges do their clients or students present? Are you aware of research that suggests certain distance-supported strategies are more effective with specific kinds of clients and needs? What kind of technology support do they have or will they need in order to offer meaningful and secure services? How will distance service impact their current work setting in terms of work flow and efficiency?

The current state of research regarding the effectiveness of Distance Counseling interventions is still evolving (Chechele & Stofle, 2003). Counselors find themselves offering distance services with care and caution because empirical research is accompanying delivery as opposed to preceding it. At the same time, Mallen (2004) suggests there is room for optimism since early exploratory research ventures are finding positive responses from counselors and clients alike. Gordon Paul's famous question regarding counseling efficacy, voiced way back in 1967 (McGowan, 2003), still applies today and raises once more this important consideration:

What works best for this particular client with this particular problem with this particular counselor in this particular setting? (p. 387)

Much of the research conducted on current Distance Counseling is anecdotal and qualitative, as is often the case during the early stages of a developing specialty. At the same time, various Distance Counseling interventions, such as the use of e-mail communication, appear to bring about positive results. Many clients report a deeper understanding of issues. Because they have time to reflect more deeply on some of the counseling insights that might be missed in the more fleeting forms of spoken communication, they are able to move towards their goals quite fluidly (Suler, 2004a; Boer, 2001). There is also considerable anecdotal evidence that supports the value of anonymity and greater privacy afforded in distance work as a catalyst for increased client self-disclosure (Chechele & Stofle, 2003). However, these same authors point out the importance of screening each client's suitability not only for distance services in general but for specifically agreed upon modalities such as chat or e-mail communication. Speaking more with respect to online therapy, they point out the need for exercising caution when dealing with individuals who present serious disorders. According to their research, Distance Counseling appears to offer some unique benefits to clients who value education and a deep understanding of issues. Clients who can work within cognitive-behavioral domains also appear to benefit from computer and technology-assisted kinds of programs to reduce anxiety and depression (Anthony, 2003).

The Clinical Case Study Group (Fenichel et al., 2002) within the International Society for Mental Health Online (2003) have presented very promising findings in an extensive report dealing with online behavior and therapeutic relationships. The article debunks several myths that challenge the possibility of working effectively with online clinical patients. The experiences and reports of these therapists provide very promising initial evidence that distance services are effective with a wide variety of clients. Although their work has been conducted mainly in the area of clinical treatment, the principles involved may be extrapolated and applied appropriately to working with clients in a career development context. Counselors and coaches also need to be aware that it is not at all uncommon for personal adjustment issues, sometimes serious ones, to emerge within the context of career planning. These exigencies make careful planning and pre-planned referral strategies an important component of any informed consent procedures covering distance services.

Lewis, Coursol, and Wahl (2004) examined the cybercounseling process from the perspectives of both client and counselor. Their findings indicate that clients do indeed benefit from the process, but that counselors need to appreciate the uniqueness of cybercounseling and adapt face-to-face interventions appropriately.

ReadyMinds' post-counseling client satisfaction surveys have yielded both quantitative and qualitative evidence that Distance Career Counseling and planning interventions within its own proprietary programs bring about effective results by adapting evidence-based, face-to-face practices via technology (Malone, Miller, & Miller, 2003). For example, ReadyMinds counselors, working via telecounseling with Internet support, use thoughtfully constructed pre-counseling questionnaires in conjunction with valid technology-supported assessment techniques in order to link clients to appropriate exploration activities. They have been able to establish meaningful counseling relationships with their clients, thus providing an ongoing support system. They employ written action plans reflecting specific goals and timetables. Their counseling program encourages thorough exploration and research of career paths including networking strategies to contact successful individuals in those career areas as models. These practices are based on comprehensive meta-analytic studies that have clearly identified successful, face-to-face career intervention strategies (Brown & Krane, 2000).

Career coaches working with either private or corporate clients as well as career or educational counselors in schools and universities have used technology to support their work for many years. Granello (2000) comments on the historical context of technology's contributions to counseling. Harris-Bowlsbey, Riley Dikel, and Sampson (2002) have offered an excellent review of this history and have provided multiple resources for counselors and clients to use. Computer assisted guidance programs (CAGS) and career information dissemination systems (CIDS) have helped individuals engage in assessment procedures and link those results to helpful sources of continued exploration. In the best of circumstances, counselors assist along the way and the client is not left alone to possibly misinterpret results or wander aimlessly from books to randomly chosen Web sites.

Over the last ten years or so, we have seen the discussion of Distance Counseling in the literature and among professionals move gradually from expressing points of view about advantages and disadvantages (Sampson, Kolodinsky, & Greeno, 1997) towards the actual implementation of programs and a critical discussion of their effectiveness. In the past, technology was seen as assisting the face-to-face counseling process through computer-assisted assessment or computer-assisted guidance activities. Technology has now become an actual delivery platform option for counseling services.

Current Research Addressing Distance Counseling Practices

One of the challenges faced by Distance Counselors is locating the ongoing empirical research that addresses the effectiveness of Distance Counseling interventions. We live in a world in which evidence-based techniques are considered the gold standard for professional services. While many clients report satisfaction with telecounseling, chat, e-mail, and video communications, more research, both quantitative and qualitative, that informs our practice in a more scientific way than simple anecdotal reports is always desirable.

Harris-Bowlsbey and Sampson (2005) present global-historical perspectives and examine current practices with respect to the use of computers and related technologies applied to career guidance and counseling. The authors speak to worldwide practices and cite specific areas of need, including the credentialing and training needs of counselors who offer Distance Counseling services.

Maheu, Pulier, Wilhelm, McMenamin, and Brown-Connolly (2005) offer a comprehensive treatment of how current communication technologies have impacted the practice of mental health professionals. Three entire chapters of their publication are devoted to online clinical practice management with a focus on salient counselor competencies in critically important areas such as technical competence, cultural literacy, communication skills, confidentiality, and security issues, to name just a few. The authors provide extensive treatment of important considerations ranging from counselor training and support to client education and care.

There have been several additional significant contributions to the research literature that provide in-depth examination of Distance Counseling services. Mallen and Vogel (2005) introduce major contributions from counseling psychology and online counseling. Their comments are followed by several thoughtful articles that examine practical aspects of online counseling. Topics include training and ethics as well as research and the trends within counseling psychology literature and practice. Jencius and Baltimore (2005) offer a comprehensive treatment of technology and contributions to cybercounseling practice, counselor education, and research. Shaw and Shaw (2006) scrutinize the important ethical issues that counselors must deal with when they deliver their services online and via additional distance modalities. This study evaluates current practices against the backdrop of various counselor association ethical standards. On the positive side, there are carefully articulated standards and guidelines provided by the various counselor associations. However, knowledge about and compliance with these standards and guidelines on the part of online counselors remains spotty; and, to quote the authors, "alarming." Far too many counselors and individuals who purport to practice counseling online simply are not aware of the standards or choose not to adhere to them in actual practice.

An earlier investigation of ethical adherence and compliance to WebCounseling (Heinlein, Welfel, Richmond, & Rak, 2003) found that, while professional counselors with licenses and degrees had a significantly higher rate of compliance than individuals with no such credentials, there was still a very low overall level of compliance with the NBCC Standards.

Admittedly, this sampling of the Web sites took place in 1999 and 2000. In addition, it examined only sites that included among its distance offerings an option for exclusively Web-based services. A much greater consciousness regarding these issues has been developing since that time, but there is still much room for improvement.

Finally, Reese, Conoley, and Brossart (2006) investigate clients' perceptions regarding the attractiveness of telecounseling. The authors report results that are very encouraging for this distance intervention. Sampled clients cite accessibility, convenience, control, and inhibition reduction as positive reasons why they found telecounseling to be a satisfying distance intervention. While these results have been reported both anecdotally and in earlier studies, this additional empirical support adds to the credibility of Distance Counseling.

The implications of these research findings challenge the counselor to become literate not only in communication technologies and systems per se, but also skilled in integrating counseling interventions with these technologies. This issue of the counselor's comfort with technology clearly raises the issue of generational membership. As Mallen (2004) points out, those individuals who have been exposed all of their lives to computers and related technology will readily adapt to distance delivered communications. Depending on experience and exposure, counselors may or may not face a more challenging learning curve.

Clearly, there are generational realities that influence an individual's exposure to and comfort with technology-related communication skills. These factors certainly play a role in each individual's readiness and comfort with respect to giving and receiving distance services. Counselors who acquired their training before the Internet revolution have certainly had to face a steeper learning curve than those who have grown up with a more immediate familiarity with the Internet and related technologies. This is not to suggest that older counselors or clients are unable or unwilling to embrace newer technology competencies. Many have done so. It is perhaps more a question of familiarity and comfort with technology influencing attitudes about the application of technology to counseling. However, we know that clients expect and are demanding that the helping professions take advantage of the advanced developments in technology that are driving many other communication strategies in our society such as healthcare and financial services. As Bloom states so clearly in his introduction to the Encore edition treatment of *Cybercounseling and Cyberlearning* (Bloom & Walz, 2004, p. xxii):

> *Our ethical duty as counselors and counselor educators is not to fight change and condemn its manifestations as being unprofessional or unethical. Rather we need to do everything in our power to embrace the benefits of change, to minimize the dangers of change, to work to eradicate the ethical dilemmas resulting from change, and to seek ways to maximize the benefits of change for our clients and students.*

While counselors should never employ counseling techniques in which they are not trained, they also need to work towards professional growth in an informed and courageous way. What we want to avoid as a profession is a form of generational, technology-resistant countertransference that rejects potentially helpful interventions to clients.

Counselors and coaches need to become competent in a whole range of Internet related electronic-technology areas ranging from encryption to Web-searching. It is clear that many of us have been using the telephone to communicate with students and clients for years. However, when conducting telecounseling more formally, they may need to pay more explicit attention to mastering the subtleties of communication with clients in scenarios where visual cues are absent. Chat sessions add the component of typing with speed while not sacrificing "visual-listening skills" to hear and speak effectively with the client.

There is also a significant challenge in learning to "write with a counseling voice" on the Internet where text is open to misunderstanding and, in fact, becomes a permanent record of counseling content. Structured training exercises in effective counselor writing skills, taken from the ReadyMinds Distance Credentialed Counselor Training Program (Malone, 2005), provide experiential activities designed to enhance the teaching of career counseling and group facilitation. The ACES technical competencies (Association for Counselor Education and Supervision, 1999) provide a useful starting point to understanding how professional counselors can integrate and master communication, information, and Internet skills within the delivery of structured and effective counseling programs. Tyler and Sabella (2004) have organized their recent publication addressing technology's contribution towards improving counseling practice around the ACES competencies, and they provide a wide array of helpful resources.

Seeking Training to Become a Distance Counselor

The recruitment, education, training, and supervision of counselors who intend to provide distance services have been ongoing professional objectives for ReadyMinds (Djadali & Malone, 2004). The Distance Credentialed Counselor (DCC) Training Program, sponsored by the Center for Credentialing in Education (CCE) and delivered by ReadyMinds, seeks to provide professional training and preparation for experienced counselors who wish to extend their skills to clients via technology-assisted counseling interventions. ReadyMinds has established a comprehensive training curriculum built around specific Distance Counselor Competencies. DCC training is currently available at locations across the United States to professionals who work in the fields of counseling, education, and coaching. Chapter Three in this book addresses the origins and development of this important partnership among ReadyMinds, the National Board for Certified Counselors, and the Center for Credentialing in Education. Please see the following link and consider this excerpt from the DCC training description on the ReadyMinds site (http://www.readyminds.com/training/dcc_cert.asp):

Distance Credentialed Counselor (DCC) Training Program

The computer and the telephone have long been invaluable tools in the workplace and in the home. It's not surprising that they have emerged as invaluable tools in the world of counseling as well. As distance methods have grown in popularity, the need for standards of practice and specialized counselor training has also grown. To address these issues, ReadyMinds, the leading provider of Distance Career Counseling and the Center for Credentialing and Education, Inc. (CCE), an affiliate of the NBCC®, is pleased to announce its Distance Credentialed Counselor (DCC) Training Program.

Distance Counseling involves some significant challenges. Even the most seasoned counselors may have concerns about engaging in distance work with their clients. These concerns might include:

• **What are the ethical issues involved in Distance Counseling?**

- **How can I build a strong working relationship with my clients via distance?**
- **How can I confirm, if I am presently practicing Distance Counseling, that I am following best practices and delivering efficient communications to my clients?**
- **What legal issues do I need to be aware of?**
- **What technology do I need for effective Distance Counseling?**

The ReadyMinds Distance Credentialed Counselor Training Program is designed to address these concerns and help counselors to incorporate distance methods into their current work settings. This 2-day, 15-hour training will provide intensive instruction in the use of distance techniques, with specific applications to career, school, and clinical counseling specialties. Topics that will be covered include:

- **What Distance Counseling "looks like"**
- **Research supporting the effectiveness of Distance Counseling**
- **Technology requirements and necessary skills**
- **Ethical and legal issues**
- **Establishing and maintaining counseling relationships "long-distance"**
- **Resolving difficult situations**

The following DCC training competencies are worthy of mention here since they address the focal point of the current chapter.

- *Counselors understand how to discuss with both colleagues and clients the various delivery models, opportunities, advantages, challenges, and professional preparation involved in the delivery of Distance Counseling services within their own specialty areas.*
- *Counselors can identify and discuss current research as well as resources that inform the practice of Distance Counseling.*
- *Counselors understand how to adapt effective face-to-face counseling techniques for application to Distance Counseling practice.*
- *Counselors understand how to relate their Distance Counseling practices and techniques to evidence based on sound theory.*

Adapting Face-to-Face Counseling Practices for Distance Counseling

Technology-supported interventions that can stand on their own or supplement face-to-face counseling relationships may include e-mail communication and/or telecounseling. Based on contact with hundreds of practicing counselors, I can report that these are usually the most favored means of conducting Distance Counseling. Depending on the available technology, as well as the skills and needs of counselor and client, videoconferencing and chat are also options. Clients may also be referred to a wide variety of computerized software programs to explore career or educational planning options as well as more therapeutic programs.

My experience as a counselor and trainer in adapting counseling techniques for distance work has reinforced my belief in the importance of structuring the counseling process and the need to focus on the stages of counseling. Whether speaking on the telephone or writing counseling e-mails, I remember to exercise appropriate counseling roles and related responses such as attending, clarifying, and supporting before moving too quickly towards informing or proscribing roles. There is an implicit tendency in distance work to move too quickly simply because technology is involved; and, in the minds of many, technology means "go fast."

A Distance Career Counseling model such as that provided by ReadyMinds demonstrates the possibility of delivering quality Distance Counseling without the initial face-to-face meetings as long as the Distance Counselor works towards establishing the counseling relationship and follows the guidelines contained in our comprehensive definition of Distance Counseling presented earlier in this chapter.

One of the central tenets in adapting effective face-to-face techniques to distance work is to always remember the stages and roles of the counseling process as described by Doyle (1992). It is essential to lay the groundwork for building the counseling relationship or working alliance. Examining the issues and coming to agreement regarding specific goals has to occur for the counseling to have meaningful outcomes for the client. Actually engaging the client in the work of the counseling comes next. Just as in face-to-face counseling, much of this work occurs between sessions beyond the cyberwalls of the virtual communication space. Finally, arriving at closure and developing a plan for aftercare as well as maintaining contact ensure ultimate comfort for the client. The following examples from the ReadyMinds Career Counseling Program illustrate both informed consent strategies and how these stages may be built into a Distance Counseling setting.

ReadyMinds Program Options

ReadyMinds recognizes that individuals tend to experience different kinds of needs and are influenced by different factors as they consider career planning. We encourage you to review all of the options offered by ReadyMinds prior to making your program choice.

ReadyMinds Informed Consent

Choosing a program that is best for you...

To assist you in understanding and selecting the ReadyMinds Program that is best for you, we have provided the following information.

Factors that influence these needs may include one or a combination of the following:
- **age and related work experience**
- **awareness of the client's interests/skills/values**
- **knowledge of how to explore and research career fields**
- **experience with decision-making about careers**
- **skills for seeking employment and/or educational placement**
- **reasons why the client is seeking career planning assistance**
- **overall experience with career planning**

Drawing from the work of Brown and Krane (2000), the ReadyMinds Counseling and Technology Teams were careful to include in their distance model the essential building blocks known to be effective in face-to-face counseling (Malone, 2002). The following strategies are examples of adapting effective in-person counseling techniques for Distance Counseling delivery:

• **A Clear and Comprehensive Web site** – so that clients may enjoy informed consent and a clear understanding of terms/conditions, fee structures, risks, and operational practices of each program.

ReadyMinds offers four distinct programs in order to meet your individual needs.

	ReadyPLATINUM	ReadyGOLD	ReadySILVER	ReadyBRONZE
1. Online Assessments				
Analysis of Your Interests, Skills, Values	✓	✓	✓	✓
2. Counselor Matching				
Personally selected ReadyMinds National Certified Counselor	✓	✓	✓	✓
Minimum Counselor Time Spent	5 hours	3 hours	2 hours	1 hour
3. One-On-One Session				
Strategies for educational and career exploration	✓	✓	✓	–
Private Interaction with RM Counselor	120 minutes via telephone	60 minutes via telephone	60 minutes via telephone	–
Assistance in educational and career decision-making	✓	✓	–	–
4. Assessment Results and Recommendations				
Written interpretive report of your Career Assessment	✓	✓	✓	✓
Self-marketing strategies: Networking, resumes, and interviewing	✓	✓	✓	–
Comprehensive Career Report and Action Plan	Insight Into U™ (4-6 page counseling report)	Guidance Summary (1-2 pages)	Guidance Summary (1-2 pages)	–
5. Ongoing Relationship				
Personal Web Page	12 months	9 months	6 months	3 months
*E-mail Access to your RM Counselor	12 months	6 months	–	–

E-mail exchange/access is intended for brief logistical communication with your counselor. Upon completion of your program you may purchase additional counselor time via telephone or private e-mail exchange.

• **A Comprehensive Registration and Assessment Protocol** – so that clients have the opportunity to state, in their own words, who they are, what their career counseling needs are and what they expect from their counseling. In addition to an open-ended questionnaire, they also complete a form of the Self-Directed Search (SDS) that is validated for Internet use. Thus, their interests, skills, and values are also available to the counselor before the actual counseling begins. This activity not only begins to build the relationship but also allows both client and counselor to explore potential issues for the counseling.

• **Personalized Selection and Assignment of a Well-Matched Counselor** – so that clients' needs may be addressed competently, and the client feels that the counselor understands the counseling issues. These factors help build trust and a strong counseling relationship.

• **Technology-Assisted Strategies and Structured Interventions** – so that clients may enjoy both convenient yet personalized communication with the counselor. Secure e-mail and planned telecounseling appointments with between-session contacts ensure continuity of service. Clients also receive pre-counseling orientation regarding the adaptations made for Distance Counseling such as assessing the client's feelings during telecounseling and related strategies to compensate for lack of visual cues. Special emphasis is placed on identifying and agreeing upon specific goals for the counseling due to the structured nature of ReadyMinds Distance Counseling Programs. The following recursive career development process serves as a means of identifying counseling needs as well as a design template for service delivery:

assessment<>exploration<>decision-making<>self-marketing

For example, client questionnaire and assessment material may suggest that the client is basically at a point of readiness in the process where specific career or educational decisions need to be made. Assuming that client self-understanding is strong and that appropriate exploration has been conducted, the counselor may suggest that the counseling and related technology-supported activities focus on actual decision-making.

• **Providing Clients with Thoughtful, Written Feedback from Their Counseling Sessions** – so that clients may enjoy a meaningful and insightful review of the counseling experience with implications for follow-up action. The distance career counselor prepares and forwards to the client a summary of the counseling contacts, which may include: stated goals, to what degree and how they were met; barriers and challenges to these goals; specific action steps as part of a plan with a timetable; and a synthesis of career assessment that is appropriately linked to resources and strategies for exploration, decision-making, and/or self-marketing. Additional research suggests that written communication provides clients and counselors with deeper insights than initially expected and enhances the career planning process in a profound way (Boer, 2001). Such a document keeps the client on course and may continue to provide motivation even after the counseling comes to a close. This documentation may also suggest strategies for post-termination follow-up communication, which enable the client and counselor to stay in touch as needed via convenient, technology-assisted Distance Counseling strategies.

• **Evaluating Distance Career Counseling Practices** – so that clients have an opportunity to express what they feel were more or less effective counseling and coaching interventions. Detailed Client Satisfaction Surveys offer opportunities for quantitative and qualitative responses about the counselor, the counseling relationship, the distance delivery model, resources, and the overall experience. This information provides valuable, critical insights so counselors and supervisors can measure effective outcomes for this new form of counseling delivery. This type of evaluation technique is especially valuable during this early phase of development for distance career counseling.

Each of these ReadyMinds program components may be replicated and adapted appropriately depending on the practice needs and work setting of counselors and their clients. Clearly, high school guidance counselors will make changes to include parents in their students' career, educational, and employment planning. There are tremendous opportunities to employ distance communication technologies with students and parents around the college admissions process. Coaches working in corporate or private settings may be more focused on employment opportunities and job search efforts although not to the exclusion of other considerations related to assessment and exploration activities.

Counselors working with special needs populations and individuals with disabilities will most certainly be engaged with assistive technologies and be familiar with the W3C World Wide Web Consortium and the related Web Accessibility Initiative. Tyler and Sabella (2004) cite several resources in their treatment of accessibility.

The following Web sites are rich resources for counselors who are seeking information about accessibility and assistive technologies: http://www.w3.org/WAI/WCAG1A-Conformance
and http://www.w3.org/WAI/EO/Drafts/PWD-Use-Web/#usage.

Basing Counseling Practices and Techniques on Evidence and Theory

Practicing counselors and coaches are well advised to take a look from time to time at the beliefs and underlying principles that guide their interventions with clients. We have all studied various theories while in training, and the durability of their importance should be apparent to us as we entertain our own answers to Gordon Paul's questions about "what works" for our clients.

Sexton (1999) echoes Paul's question that calls for evidence-based counseling in the preparation and practice of professional counselors. The process of conducting research to inform specific practice interventions is an ongoing mandate in the interests of client care, especially when working with an evolving specialty such as Distance Counseling.

Osipow's continuous imperative to apply the practical implications of theory to practice (1968, 1973, 1983; Osipow & Fitzgerald, 1995) and a systems approach to career development theory (Patton & McMahon, 1999) have consistently provided guiding principles for my work as a counselor and counselor educator.
Based on this genre of literature as well as my own professional experience, the following benefits of theory-based counseling are apparent to me:

- *A context for the understanding and interpretation of client issues.* Theories provide a context in which the counselor can understand and interpret the issues and questions the client brings to the counseling situation.

- *A descriptive blueprint that explains adaptive behaviors.* Theories offer a descriptive blueprint that explains how people engage in adaptive behaviors and make choices both during specific life-stage periods as well as over the entire lifespan.

- *Useful counseling intervention strategies supported by empirical research.* Theories can provide practitioners with useful counseling intervention strategies when supported by empirical studies.

- *Eclectic integration of theories.* Theories differ in their relative emphasis of certain variables, usually due to the professional field/point of view/bias of the theorist. However, many theories share common beliefs and allow for integration, even if on a limited basis.

- *Systematic and client-appropriate application of theory based interventions.* Theories can provide especially effective interventions for practitioners when their empirically supported counseling techniques are aligned with the belief system/culture of the client, applied systematically in an integrated program and delivered within the working alliance of a strong counseling relationship.

Goss and Anthony (2003) raise several compelling issues regarding the need for research:
- evolution of evidence in innovative areas of counseling
- comparative evidence among various Distance Counseling models
- challenge of delivering services while conducting research
- who is most suitable to receive/deliver Distance Counseling?
- anecdotal and empirical bases of research evidence

There are frequent reports from the field regarding contributions of Distance Counseling. The intriguing question here is whether some Distance Counseling interventions are unique precisely because of the technology-assisted factor. That is, can Distance Counseling provide some benefits that face-to-face delivery cannot? Certainly we are uncovering evidence that there are unique advantages to Distance Counseling such as convenience, efficiency, and comfort-of-experience for certain kinds of clients who prosper in the distance relationship because they prefer relative anonymity. Fenichel et al. (2002) address the important point, the need for "a theory of cybertherapy," when speaking about the comparison of online and offline principles that guide counselors and therapists in their work. His team speaks to the need for such a "theory" while addressing the myth that online principles are the same as offline principles.

Case studies and reports from the perspectives of client and counselor/therapist continue to support the mandate for further research. It would be especially useful to examine not only client reactions, but also the feelings and convictions of the counselors and coaches on the front lines who have delivered these services. ReadyMinds has conducted ongoing debriefing of their clients and counselors using both quantitative and qualitative questionnaire protocols. A substantial percentage of responding clients have cited a personalized and meaningful counselor relationship as the most important outcome within their distance career counseling experience. Overall, client feedback has been encouraging, and the constructive and positive criticisms from both sides of the process have provided valuable insights that have been used to improve ReadyMinds program design and service delivery. Counselors express high levels of satisfaction with their distance work. Among the most frequently mentioned advantages are convenience, efficiency, and the ability to move clients towards their goals due to the carefully designed delivery of services.

Who are the counselors and coaches we might expect to function best in the distance arena? What personal qualities and skills should a client seek from a professional offering distance services? Who are the best candidates for training? Chapter Four will address these and several related questions.

Counselor Tips for Taking Action

- *Provide clients and colleagues with clear explanations regarding the rationale for and delivery of Distance Counseling services by discussing appropriately selected elements from the comprehensive definition of Distance Counseling provided in this chapter.*
- *Choose specific Distance Counseling delivery strategies and design well-structured Distance Counseling models based on your scope of practice, work setting, and the needs of your clients.*
- *Stay current with respect to past and evolving research in the field in order to inform your practice and work with clients.*
- *Pay consistent attention to Gordon Paul's famous question: "What works best for this particular client with this particular problem with this particular counselor in this particular setting?"*
- *Acquire the necessary technical skills and support systems in order to deliver secure distance services to your clients.*
- *Seek appropriate training, both formal and informal, in order to become competent in delivering Distance Counseling.*

- *Employ clearly written and well designed Web sites, print materials, pre-counseling questionnaires, and post-counseling services in order to communicate effectively with your clients.*
- *Make the technical and counseling adaptations necessary to working with special needs clients.*
- *Seek evaluation from your clients with respect to the effectiveness of your distance services, and engage in consistent analysis regarding the effectiveness of your distance techniques*
- *Seek ongoing support from your supervisors and esteemed colleagues in order to ensure the best Distance Counseling care to your clients*

Questions for Chapter Review

1. How does the comprehensive definition of Distance Counseling impact on me as a counselor or coach in light of my work setting and scope of practice?
2. What is the best way for me to explain to my clients and colleagues the specific distance services I plan to offer? Indeed, which specific forms of Distance Counseling will I offer?
3. What is my current knowledge and skill level with respect to Distance Counseling, and how can I gain further training?
4. Where will I find current resources and research to support my distance practices?
5. How can I effectively adapt my face-to-face techniques for distance application, and what are some of the unique benefits that distance work can offer to me and my clients?
6. How shall I design my distance service offerings or program so clients may enjoy informed consent and a clear understanding of what they will be experiencing?
7. How will I seek evidence of success with my clients and evaluate the effectiveness of my distance services?

References

Association for Counselor Education and Supervision. (1999). *ACES technical competencies for counselor education students, 1999.* Retrieved November 25, 2003 from http://filebox.vt.edu/users/thohen/competencies.htm

Anthony, K. (2003). The use and role of technology in counseling and psychotherapy. In S. Goss & K. Anthony (Eds.), *Technology in counseling and psychotherapy: A practitioner's guide* (pp. 13-35). Houndmills, UK: Palgrave Macmillan.

Bloom, J., & Walz, G. (2000). (Eds.). *Cybercounseling and cyberlearning: Strategies and resources for the millennium.* Alexandria, VA: American Counseling Association.

Bloom, J. W., & Walz, G. R. (Eds.). (2004). *Cybercounseling and cyberlearning: An encore.* Greensboro, NC: CAPS Press.

Boer, P. (2001). *Career counseling over the internet: An emerging model for trusting and responding to online clients.* Mahwah, NJ: Lawrence Erlbaum Associates.

Brown, S. D., & Krane, R. N. (2000). Four (or five) sessions and a cloud of dust: Old assumptions and new observations about career counseling. In S. D. Brown & R. W. Lent (Eds.), *Handbook of counseling psychology* (pp.740-766). New York: John Wiley & Sons.

Chechele, P. J., & Stofle, G. (2003). Individual therapy online via e-mail and Internet relay chat. In S. Goss & K. Anthony (Eds.), *Technology in counseling and psychotherapy: A practitioner's guide* (pp. 39-58). Houndmills, UK: Palgrave Macmillan.

Djadali, Y., & Malone, J. F. (2004). Distance career counseling: A technology-assisted model for delivering career counseling services. In Garry R. Walz & Chris Kirkman (Eds.), *CyberBytes: Highlighting compelling issues of technology in counseling* (pp. 7-16). Greensboro, NC: CAPS Publications.

Doyle, J. (1992). *Essential skills and strategies in the helping process.* Belmont, CA: Wadsworth.

Fenichel, M., Suler, J., Barak, A., Zelvin, E., Jones, G., Munro, K., Meunier, V., & Walker-Schmucker, W. (2002). *Myths and realities of online clinical work.* Retrieved September 23, 2005, from http://www.rider.edu/~suler/psycyber/ myths.html

Goss, S., & Anthony, K. (Eds.). (2003). *Technology and counseling in psychotherapy.* Houndsmills, England: Palgrave Macmillan.

Granello, P. F. (2000). Historical context: The relationship of computer technologies and counseling. In J. W. Bloom & G. R. Walz, (Eds.), Cybercounseling and cyberlearning: Strategies and resources for the millennium. Alexandria, VA: American Counseling Association.

Harris-Bowlsbey, J., Riley Dikel, M., & Sampson, J. P., Jr. (2002). *The Internet: A tool for career planning.* Tulsa, OK: National Career Development Association.

Harris-Bowlsbey, J., & Sampson, J. P., Jr. (2005). Use of technology in delivering career services worldwide. *The Career Development Quarterly, 54,* 48-56.

Heinlein, K. T., Welfel, E. R., Richmond, E. N., & Rak, C. F. (2003). The scope of WebCounseling: A survey of services and compliance with NBCC standards for the ethical practice of WebCounseling. *Journal of Counseling and Development, 81,* 61-69.

International Society for Mental Health Online. (2003). *Assessing a person's suitability for online therapy.* Retrieved November 25, 2003 from http://ismho.org/casestudy/ccsgas.htm

Jencius, M., & Baltimore, M. (Eds.). (2005). *The Journal of Technology in Counseling, 4(1).* Retrieved June 8, 2006, from http://jtc.colstate.edu/Vol4_1/Index.htm

Lewis, J., Coursol, D., & Herting Wahl, K. (2004). Researching the cybercounseling process: A study of the client and counselor experience. In J. W. Bloom & G. R. Walz (Eds.), *Cybercounseling and cyberlearning: An encore.* Greensboro, NC: CAPS Press.

Maheu, M. M., Pulier, M. L, Wilhelm, F. H, McMenamin, J. P., & Brown-Connolly, N. E. (2005). *The mental health professional and the new technologies: A handbook for practice today.* Mahwah, NJ: Lawrence Erlbaum Associates.

Mallen, M. J. (2004). Online counseling research. In R.Kraus, J. Zack, & G. Stricker (Eds.), *Online counseling: A handbook for mental health professionals.* San Diego, CA: Elsevier Academic Press.

Mallen, M. J., & Vogel, D. L. (2005). Online counseling: Challenges for the information era. *The Counseling Psychologist, 53*(6), 776-818.

Malone, J. F. (2002). *Working towards effective practices in distance career counseling* (ERIC Digest EDO-CG-02 03). Greensboro, NC: ERIC Counseling and Student Services. (ERIC Document Reproduction Service No. EDCG032075)

Malone, J. F. (2005). Asynchronous distance career counseling communication technique. In C. W. Minor & M. Pope (Eds.), *Experiential activities for teaching career counseling classes and for facilitating career groups, Volume 2.* Tulsa, OK: National Career Development Association.

Malone, J. F., Miller, K. S., & Miller, R. M. (2003). The evolution of a distance career counseling model: Implications for training, practice and supervision of cybercounselors. In J. W. Bloom & G. R. Walz (Eds.), *Cybercounseling & cyberlearning: An encore.* Greensboro, NC: ACA Foundation & CAPS Publications.

McGowan, A. S. (2003). New and practical sections in the Journal of Counseling & Development: Information for the prospective author and the readership. Journal of Counseling & Development, 81, 387.

National Board for Certified Counselors. (2001). *The Practice of Internet Counseling.* Retrieved November 24, 2003, from http://www.nbcc.org/ethics/webethics.htm

Osipow, S. H. (1968, 1973, 1983). *Theories of career development* (1st, 2nd & 3rd ed.). Englewood Cliffs, NJ: Prentice-Hall, Inc.

Osipow, S. H., & Fitzgerald, L. F. (1996). *Theories of career development* (4th ed.). Boston: Allyn & Bacon.

Patton, W., & McMahon, M. (1999). *Career development and systems theory: A new relationship.* Pacific Grove, CA: Brooks/Cole Publishing Company.

ReadyMinds, LLC. (2004). *Distance Credentialed Counselor (DCC) training program and credential.* Retrieved April 10, 2006, from http://www.readyminds.com/training/dcc_cert.asp

ReadyMinds, LLC. (2003). *ReadyMinds program options & informed consent.* Retrieved April 10, 2006, from http://www.readyminds.com/cc/options/overview.asp

Reese, R. J., Conoley, C. W., Brossart, D. F. (2006). The attractiveness of telephone counseling: An empirical investigation of client perceptions. *The Journal of Counseling & Development, 84,* 54-60.

Rosenfield, M. (1997). *Counseling by telephone.* Thousand Oaks, CA: Sage Publications.

Sampson, J. P., Jr., Kolodinsky, R. W., & Greeno, B. P. (1997). Counseling on the information highway: Future possibilities and potential problems. *Journal of Counseling & Development, 75,* 203-212.

Sexton, T. L. (1999). *Evidence-based counseling: Implications for counseling practice, preparation, and professionalism.* Greensboro, NC: ERIC Counseling and Student Services. (ERIC Document Reproduction Service No. ED 435948)

Shaw, H. E. & Shaw, S. F. (2006). Critical ethical issues in online counseling: Assessing current practices with an ethical intent checklist. *Journal of Counseling & Development, 84,* 41-53.

Shy, J. D., & Sampson, J. P. (2005). *Distance counseling bibliography*. Retrieved September 23, 2005 from http://www.career.fsu.edu/documents/bibliographies/Distance%20 Counseling_7_21.htm

Suler, J. (2004a). *Psychotherapy in cyberspace.* Retrieved September 23, 2005 from http://www.rider.edu/~suler/psycyber/therapy.html

Suler, J. (2004b). *The online disinhibition effect.* Retrieved September 23, 2005 from http://www.rider.edu/users/suler/psycyber/disinhibit.html

Tyler, J. M., & Sabella, R. (2004). *Using technology to improve counseling practice.* Alexandria, VA: American Counseling Association.

CHAPTER THREE

The Distance Credentialed Counselor

Susan P. Shafer and Thomas W. Clawson

This chapter provides a brief history of the development of the National Board for Certified Counselors (NBCC) and the Center for Credentialing and Education (CCE) and discusses the differences among certification, credentialing, licensure, and registration. The development of the Distance Credentialed Counselor (DCC) certification and the requirements for DCC certification are presented, followed by a discussion of the benefits and advantages of DCC certification.

With a population of approximately 300 million in the United States and just over 200,000 counselors, the need for better counselor access is evident, especially in rural areas. As technology has advanced, Distance Counseling has become a reality. With this reality came a new need for quality standards aimed at protecting the public. The Center for Credentialing and Education (CCE), an affiliate of the National Board for Certified Counselors, established eligibility requirements to help identify to the public those individuals who have met substantial standards necessary for the practice and delivery of Distance Counseling. Having established the standards for Distance Counseling in 1998, CCE's parent company, the National Board for Certified Counselors (NBCC), was aware of CCE's business activities and the impending needs.

The National Board for Certified Counselors

The National Board for Certified Counselors (NBCC) was established in 1982 as a not-for-profit credentialing body for counselors. With over 38,000 certified counselors, NBCC is the largest certifier of professional counselors in the world.

NBCC was initially developed after the work of a committee of the American Counseling Association (ACA). ACA later created NBCC to be an independent credentialing body. NBCC and ACA have strong historical ties, and both work to further the profession of counseling with separate and distinct missions and goals. ACA focuses on membership association activities such as conferences, professional development, publications, and government relations. NBCC focuses primarily on promoting quality counseling through certification to individuals, and private and government organizations; however, many areas of counselor and client advocacy are embedded in their work on standards of practice. NBCC is accredited by the National Commission for Certifying Agencies (NCCA) and is one of less than 50 accredited certifying agencies in existence.

The Center for Credentialing and Education

The Center for Credentialing and Education (CCE) is a corporate affiliate of NBCC established in 1997. NBCC initially created CCE to develop and manage credentialing and related programs both within mental health and outside the professional counseling arena. CCE has since grown to provide quality services to organizations, educational institutions, and governmental agencies including association and board management services and examination services, as well as credential review and management services. For example, as a contracted agent of several state counselor licensure boards, CCE is the initial point of entry for those applying for licensure in those particular states.

CCE also offers products and services directly to counselors and other mental health professionals including study course materials, online counseling education, and professional credentials. One of CCE's largest credentials is the Global Career Development Facilitator (GCDF). The GCDF curriculum enables trained facilitators to apply basic psychological and sociological principles along with labor market information to help individuals maintain a healthy balance of work, family, and leisure. The credential, which originally grew out of a governmental grant, has developed a strong international base and is now in use or under development in several different countries including Japan, New Zealand, Turkey, Canada, China, Germany, and Romania.

Certification as a Form of Credentialing

Many confuse the terms licensure, registration, and certification, primarily because there is some overlap among the three, all of which are forms of credentialing. Licensure generally refers to the mandatory governmental requirement for an individual to practice in a particular profession and particular jurisdiction. Registration is normally a mandatory process governed by a governmental or private agency and usually requires an individual to only apply or register to be on record as practicing in a particular jurisdiction. Finally, certification is usually a voluntary process instituted by a nongovernmental agency in which individuals are recognized for substantial knowledge and skill (National Organization for Competency Assurance, 1996).

As indicated earlier, CCE is a certification body whose primary focus is professional voluntary certification. By conducting its certification programs, CCE has the responsibility of designing programs that will help ensure that the certified and competent practitioner performs work accurately and in the best interest of those served, while also making correct judgments. A strong ethics enforcement program is critical in this respect.

Development of DCC Certification

In collaboration with ReadyMinds Corporation, the leading provider of distance career counseling, CCE worked to define the practice of Distance Counseling. A CCE expert panel reviewed and approved the comprehensive training package developed by ReadyMinds as the required training for all Distance Credentialed Counselors (DCCs). Additionally, a professional counselor focus group established the standards and requirements for the credential. This group, with expert opinion and research, established the fundamental requirements and competency that an individual would need to meet for successful Distance Counseling practice. This included the establishment of education, standards of ethical practice, continuing education requirements, and training that closely matched the existing training given by ReadyMinds. Current certification and licensure standards that have been developed scientifically over the past three decades added to the strength of the DCC requirements.

Requirements for DCC Certification

DCCs have an earned Master's degree in counseling or a related field from a regionally accredited college or university. In addition, DCCs are certified in good standing as a National Certified Counselor (NCC), or are licensed to practice counseling, or licensed in a related field in the state where the DCC resides or works.

DCCs have successfully completed the two-day, 15 hour Distance Counselor Training Program offered by ReadyMinds. This training takes place after the individual has practiced as a professional. The training covers such areas as:

- the rationale for Distance Counseling services;
- building a strong working relationship using Distance Counseling methods;
- planning and stages within Distance Counseling relationships;
- how to incorporate Distance Counseling methods within the current work setting;
- Distance Counseling case management;
- ethical and legal issues;
- approaches to difficult situations;
- technology methods and assessing outcomes and client satisfaction (ReadyMinds, 2004).

DCCs have signed an attestation that they will comply with the most current NBCC *Code of Ethics* and the NBCC *Ethical Requirements for the Practice of Internet Counseling*. Both codes were adopted by CCE for the DCC credential. Counselors are prepared to ethically deliver counseling as long as the specific counseling services they offer are congruent with their education, training, and supervised experience (National Board for Certified Counselors, 2002).

To maintain their credential, DCCs document 20 hours of workshop, in-service training, conference attendance or coursework over a five-year certification period. All hours must be focused in a counseling or mental health related area, and five of the hours must be specifically focused on Distance Counseling.

Benefits of DCC Certification

Professional certification carries many purposes. First, it helps clarify to the public those professionals who are qualified to perform this specialized work. Second, it aids in the networking of DCCs for themes such as peer supervision, idea sharing, and client referral. Third, it sets an ethical standard that DCCs must strictly follow. Fourth, it helps to facilitate the growth of the practice where standards can be re-explored.

United States Law and Practice

DCC certification does not supersede U.S. practice laws that are in effect in most states. Counselor licensure is now in force in 48 states (only California and Nevada do not have regulation of counselors). Most of the states have statutes in place that require an individual to practice only in the jurisdiction in which they hold active licensure. The advent of Distance Counseling and the ease of practicing across state lines have caused many states to explore their laws to determine where the jurisdiction ends. DCC ethical guidelines require that the certificant adhere to state requirements wherever they are providing services, which through Distance Counseling extends to where the client is.

The practice of Distance Counseling can become more complicated through international use. On the positive side, Distance Counseling may provide greater access for individuals living abroad especially U.S. nationals. However, questions of licensure and jurisdiction also come into question in a world filled with countries where professional counseling does not exist, or exists with no licensure laws in place. Additionally, challenges also come into play with international use of Distance Counseling in terms of taxes and currency. In short, we can expect some more barriers to practice with every national or international boundary we cross.

The newly established DCC is future oriented because it lends itself to greater portability across the states and to global use. Although the practice opens the door to just as many questions as answers, the training and standards put in place through such a credential are an important historic landmark for a future reality in the practice of counseling. Confidence in ReadyMinds was built prior to partnering. Both CCE and ReadyMinds have made appropriate service delivery a top priority and will continue to explore and refine standards as portability of counseling professionals continues to grow and as the use of Distance Counseling continues to expand across state and national borders.

References

Center for Credentialing and Education. (2004). *DCC Application*. Retrieved October 27,2004, from http://www.cce-global.org/pdfs/DCCApplication.pdf.

National Board for Certified Counselors. (2002). *Code of Ethics*. Retrieved October 26, 2004, from http://www.nbcc.org/pdfs/ethics/NBCC-CodeofEthics.pdf.

National Board for Certified Counselors and the Center for Credentialing and Education. (2001). *The practice of Internet counseling*. Retrieved October 26, 2004, from http://www.nbcc.org/ethics/webethics.htm.

National Organization for Competency Assurance. (1996). *Certification: A NOCA Handbook*. Washington, DC: NOCA.

ReadyMinds. (2004). *Distance Credentialed Counselor (DCC) Training Program and Credential*. Retrieved October 4, 2004, from http://www.readyminds.com/training/dcc_cert.asp.

CHAPTER FOUR

Who Can Perform Distance Counseling?

DeeAnna Merz Nagel

This chapter begins with a definition of counseling in the context of Distance Counseling and assists the reader in conceptualizing how Distance Counseling may be delivered. Taking into consideration legal and ethical issues that are further discussed in Chapter Eleven, the skills and mindset necessary to deliver Distance Counseling services are discussed. Comparisons of Distance Counseling with existing theories regarding the stages and process of counseling are reviewed. Finally, necessary prerequisites to becoming an educated and competent Distance Counselor are offered.

Sue is a career counselor in private practice. One weekend per month she volunteers at a local domestic violence shelter and answers the hotline. She is convinced that telecounseling with individuals in crisis is effective and begins to wonder how she might utilize her skills in her private practice. She asks herself the following questions:

- *If people have been using hotlines effectively for years, could similar benefits apply to other forms of counseling with people who are not necessarily in crisis?*
- *Are there any organizations or companies in existence that already use telephones and the Internet to provide counseling services?*
- *Do I possess the skills necessary to counsel people about their careers via the telephone and related distance methods?*
- *Has research been conducted regarding the efficacy of Distance Counseling?*
- *What other forms of technology are professionals using to provide counseling services?*
- *Where can I go for additional information and training?*

Distance Counseling

In this era of technology, Distance Counseling is not an unusual occurrence. One must consider all the various forms Distance Counseling might take and the abundance of caveats within each form. For instance, Distance Counseling may take place via letter (snail mail) and telephone. These formats are certainly not new and do not necessarily fit into today's technological definition of Distance Counseling, but no one would argue that distance is involved. Online counseling, another form of Distance Counseling, may include various forms such as e-mail, chat, bulletin board or forum posts, blogs, video conferencing, and other forms of communication utilizing Internet technology.

When first considering who can perform Distance Counseling, a definition of counseling and/or psychotherapy should be established. Counseling is defined by Merriam-Webster as follows:

> *professional guidance of the individual by utilizing psychological methods especially in collecting case history data, using various techniques of the personal interview, and testing interests and aptitudes*

Psychotherapy is defined by the same dictionary as follows:

> *treatment of mental or emotional disorder or of related bodily ills by psychological means*

Given these definitions, it becomes clear that counseling includes a professional skill set, and psychotherapy is further defined in terms of the provision of treatment. These factors are important when one considers who can perform counseling of any kind, including Distance Counseling.

In addition, each state may have different definitions of counseling under licensing laws that further clarify the scope of practice for counselors. Depending on whether the state offers practice protection through a title law, a person may not even be permitted to utilize the terms *counselor/counseling* or *therapist/psychotherapy* without the appropriate license to do so.

Another issue to consider is the setting in which certain licensing laws may not apply. These settings usually include government settings and school settings. Generally, a person can receive counseling through a government mental health agency, and a licensed person may or may not be employed onsite. Similarly, a school may be able to provide guidance or career counseling without a licensed person available at the setting. Generally, however, counselors in educational settings have to satisfy state certification requirements that differ from a formal license.

Clearly, before consideration is given to the provision of counseling, one must become aware of the laws and practices within his or her jurisdiction and take into account the setting in which the provision of counseling will take place. But beyond acting in compliance with legal and ethical mandates, what are some of the traits possessed by counselors who really can perform Distance Counseling?

To approach an answer to this central question, let us consider some additional factors with respect to how Distance Counseling takes place and relates to face-to-face counseling. Distance Counseling should not be considered a theory of counseling or a format that utilizes a certain technique. Rather, distance is another way in which the counseling is delivered. For instance, individual, couples, family, and group counseling all provide a different way in which the counseling is delivered. The counseling may be delivered with one facilitator or more; the counseling may be delivered in an office setting. Perhaps the counseling is delivered in a home setting, if the services are part of a child welfare agency intervention. The counseling services may be delivered in a shelter setting (e.g., battered women, homeless individuals) or a group home setting (e.g., adolescents, adults with developmental disabilities). But, regardless of any of the aforementioned delivery situations and settings, a variety of techniques and theories can be utilized. The same professional choices apply to the delivery of counseling services via distance.

Another way to conceptualize the difference between counseling that is delivered face-to-face versus distance is delineated by the National Board for Certified Counselors (2005) in *The Taxonomy for Defining Face-to Face and Technology-Assisted Distance Counseling*, which was described in Chapter Two. Participants in counseling can be individuals, couples, or groups, while the location for counseling delivery can be face-to-face or via distance, assisted by technology. Whether the communication is read, heard, or seen is a function of the communication medium.

It should be noted that each method of delivery mentioned above generally requires a different set of training and skills. A combination of participants, location, and medium can affect the skill necessary to deliver counseling effectively. Many counselors and therapists can conduct counseling using either an individual or group format, but they have generally had some additional training and education in the provision of group counseling. In another instance, a counselor who has delivered guidance counseling to students in a traditional school setting could decide to expand by delivering similar services in a private practice setting. While the counselor may have excellent counseling skills and be accustomed to pulling from a variety of theories, it is wise for the counselor to obtain additional training before providing services privately since a variety of new challenges may accompany the change. Likewise, a counselor who wants to offer services via distance should obtain additional training that would support existing skills with the necessary adaptations and enhance delivery of services via distance.

Some would say the most obvious difference between traditional counseling and Distance Counseling is the lack of paralinguistic and visual cues. However, some Distance Counseling formats such as phone and video conferencing allow for, if not one, both cues. Chat components via the Internet now allow for typing, visual, and talking to occur simultaneously. It becomes clear that different forms of Distance Counseling can have their own host of nuances.

So how does one "get started?" For some in the counseling field, embracing Distance Counseling is a natural offshoot to existing face-to-face techniques that have something in common with distance delivery. For example:

- If a counselor has worked a telephone hotline, that counselor has already experienced the lack of visual cues and the quick rapport and disclosure from clients that often occurs during Distance Counseling.
- Deciding to provide counseling services via telephone does not become such a leap.
- For counselors who have offered "advice" through help columns in newspapers or magazines, the idea of offering similar services via e-mail exchange is another transferable skill.
- Some counselor educators who have taught classes utilizing satellite technology might not find real-time video counseling such a stretch from their current skill-set.

- Counselor educators who view therapy sessions via video or who listen to recordings of sessions are familiar with the nuances related to technology such as interpreting inflection. This individual would likely be able to adjust to similar issues that occur using technology during a counseling session.
- Career counselors who assist school alumni via e-mail and find themselves dipping into career counseling issues may find e-mail intervention to be an effective strategy for career counseling concerns.
- Psychotherapists often recommend journaling as a part of the therapy process. Such practitioners might find the use of e-mail (Childress, 1999) and most recently, blogs, a perfect segue into the use of technology to enhance the therapeutic process.
- Bibliotherapy is a technique that is utilized by counselors of all types. For counselors who use the written word to engage clients, the Internet can open many new and fresh avenues (Barak, 1999).

These are but a few examples of transferable experiences that might aid a counselor in determining his or her comfort level with regard to Distance Counseling. Other issues that determine whether Distance Counseling is a practical delivery choice for a counselor are a counselor's comfort level with use of the written word in absence of paralinguistic cues, how accustomed a counselor is to the Internet, computers and technology in general, and actual skill level such as typing or grammar (Zelvin & Speyer, 2004). It is also important for potential Distance Counselors to consider their tolerance for ambiguity and, once again, their comfort level in engaging in a new, evolving specialty within the profession.

All of that aside, the key to providing effective Distance Counseling is directly related to the counselor and client's investment in the process. As with any prescribed counseling technique, Distance Counseling should be structured to allow for the necessary components of service. A skilled Distance Counselor knows how to sculpt time and sessions with the client. In the delivery of successful career counseling via distance, ReadyMinds (Malone, Miller, & Ravis, 2003) describes six stages in the Distance Counseling process:

1. Building trust and establishing the Distance Counseling relationship
2. Preparing the client to participate successfully in Distance Counseling work

3. Exploring issues and establishing goals in Distance Counseling
4. Strategies for "doing the work" in Distance Counseling
5. Communication procedures between sessions
6. Termination and follow-up contacts.

These six stages follow closely the already existing beliefs regarding the structured stages of face-to-face counseling. One can conclude that if a counselor can embrace the idea that counseling can be delivered via technology and has successful skills in technology-related counseling techniques that facilitate rapport building, assessment, treatment, and termination of the counseling process, then Distance Counseling is likely a viable medium for that individual.

Once a counselor has decided that Distance Counseling is a medium that is worth pursuing, how does the counselor gain the appropriate knowledge and experience? Proper training is essential. Although some training courses offer a fundamental review of various topics such as telephone etiquette or e-mail/chat exchange, they may be rudimentary and basic. It is paramount that these skills be integrated into the Distance Counseling experience in a systematic and comprehensive way.

Many professional counseling and psychology organizations have developed guidelines and codes of ethics (American Counseling Association, 2005; American Mental Health Counselor Association, 2004; American Psychological Association, 2002; International Society for Mental Health Online, 2000; National Board of Certified Counselors, 2005) regarding the provision of Distance Counseling. However, there exists no universal set of skills that a Distance Counselor must possess. This is not unlike other quagmires in the helping professions such as license portability or the difference between national certification and state licensure. The task of the professional is to seek out the more revered and respected roads to travel within a certain specialty, especially an evolving one such as Distance Counseling. Fortunately, the Distance Credentialed Counselor (DCC) Training Program is now available for counseling professionals who wish to establish a certain set of competencies in a formal way. The DCC credential is offered through the Center for Credentialing in Education (CCE), an affiliate of the National Board for Certified Counselors (NBCC) and ReadyMinds. For counselors who are new to the idea of Distance Counseling, the DCC training and credentialing process provides a viable method to achieve the knowledge necessary for skilled delivery of services; and it includes training in a comprehensive list of Distance Counseling competencies.

Once the knowledge has been acquired, the next step involves utilizing existing skills and integrating new skills learned through training. Experience must be gained as confidence is built and competent services are delivered. Clinical supervision and/or case consultation may be necessary to develop the appropriate skill levels in Distance Counseling. Peer supervision/consultation is a viable resource for building competency. Joining organizations that will keep the counselor abreast of ongoing research and new information is essential. The key components to becoming a seasoned Distance Counselor are summarized below:

1. Acquire knowledge, both rudimentary and advanced, via formal training such as the DCC Program, continuing education courses (online and face-to-face), professional journals, and other written materials.
2. Consider a certification that will demonstrate your proficiencies publicly.
3. Integrate existing knowledge and skills with newly acquired knowledge and skills.
4. Consider ongoing clinical supervision or case consultation on a case-by-case basis.
5. Engage in peer supervision/consultation.
6. Join organizations that offer peer support and/or disseminate new knowledge and advances in Distance Counseling.

Finally, once skill and experience are acquired, contributing to the field of Distance Counseling should be considered. This can be accomplished by mentoring other Distance Counselors new to the field, adding to the existing body of qualitative and quantitative literature on the topic of Distance Counseling, and providing education, when appropriate, to legislative bodies, licensing boards, and Counselor Educators.

Closing Remarks

In summary, determining who can perform Distance Counseling requires consideration of a number of issues. First, one must determine if he or she is qualified under existing codes and laws to conduct counseling of any type. Second, the counselor must explore whether the use of distance technology would be a good "fit." Third, once a fit has been determined, the counselor must take inventory of existing skills and acquire new skills relevant to Distance Counseling. Fourth, the counselor must then apply the knowledge and skill to gain experience. Finally, once skill and competence are obvious, the Distance Counselor should consider contributing to the field of Distance Counseling.

Counselor Tips for Taking Action

- *Acquire a clear and solid understanding of how Distance Counseling delivery differs from face-to-face counseling techniques.*
- *Acquire knowledge and understanding of the various modalities of Distance Counseling: telecounseling, e-mail, chat, video-assisted, and stand-alone software.*
- *Relate these various modalities to specific kinds of clients and their counseling needs.*
- *Relate your own communication and counseling skills to each of these modalities to choose those that suit you best.*
- *Understand the ethical, legal, and regulatory guidelines that apply to Distance Counseling.*
- *Identify your training needs and seek training in any of the following areas: active listening for telecounselin; insightful reading for e-mail and chat; writing in an effective counseling style for e-mail and chat; or overall technology skills for use on the Internet or in video-counseling.*

Questions and Scenarios for Chapter Review

1. You offer a parenting advice column in a local newspaper in addition to a private practice specializing in family therapy. What transferable skills exist that could aid you in your decision to offer Distance Counseling?

2. You are a career counselor at a busy university offering face-to-face services. When you are home, one of your favorite ways to relax and feel connected is to use instant message chat with your

close friends and family. How can you apply this skill to Distance Counseling? What would be similar or different?

3. You are computer savvy, using e-mail, bulletin boards, and chat on a daily basis. You are a counselor educator and utilize the computer on a daily basis to communicate with students and do research. You think you have the skills necessary to become a Distance Counselor. Why would you necessarily benefit from education about Distance Counseling?

4. You are a licensed counselor and your state has a provision that allows you to conduct Distance Counseling as long as you practice within state borders. Why should you consider additional credentialing in Distance Counseling?

5. You have provided Distance Counseling from home for several years and teach part-time at a local college. Several students who are near completion of their advanced degree in counseling have expressed interest in Distance Counseling. How can you contribute to the body of knowledge that already exists and mentor future Distance Counselors?

References

American Counseling Association. (2005). *ACA code of ethics*, 2005. Retreived October 5, 2005, from http://www.counseling.org/Resources/CodeOfEthics/TP/Home/CT2.aspx?

American Mental Health Counselor Association. (2004). *Principle 14: Internet on-line counseling*. Retrieved October 6, 2005, from http://www.amhca.org/code/#14

American Psychological Association. (2002). *Ethics code.* Retrieved October 6, 2005, from http://www.apa.org/ethics/.

Barak, A. (1999). Psychological applications on the Internet: A discipline on the threshold of a new millennium. *Applied and Preventive Psychology*, 8, 231-246.

Childress, C. A. (1999). Interactive e-mail journals: A model of providing psychotherapeutic intervention using the Internet. *CyberPsychology & Behavior*, 2, 213-221.

International Society for Mental Health Online. (2000). *Suggested principles for the online provision of mental health services.* Retrieved June 13, 2006, from http://www.ismho.org/suggestions.html.

Malone, J. F., Miller, K. S., & Ravis, H. (2003). *ReadyMinds distance credentialed counselor training handbook.* Internal Proprietary Training Document. Lyndhurst, NJ: Ready & Motivated Minds, LLC.

National Board for Certified Counselors. (2005). *The practice of Internet counseling.* Retrieved October 5, 2005, from http://www.nbcc.org/webethics2.

Zelvin, E., & Speyer, C. M. (2004). Online counseling skills, Part 1: Treatment strategies and skills for conducting counseling online. In R. Kraus, J. Zack, & G. Stricker (Eds.), *Online counseling: A handbook for mental health professionals* (pp. 163-180). San Diego, CA: Elsevier Academic Press.

CHAPTER FIVE

The Assessment Process via Distance Counseling

Jill Lumsden

This chapter discusses the use of career assessment as part of Distance Counseling services. Advantages and potential limitations of distance career assessment are described. The ReadyMinds model of distance assessment is provided as a successful example of incorporating assessment into the distance counseling services. Finally, strategies for incorporating distance assessment into your delivery of Distance Counseling services are explored.

The following two student situations provide a description of career assessment and counseling services offered in a traditional face-to-face format as compared with a distance delivery model.

Mark comes into his community college career center and sets up an appointment to see a counselor. He has to wait three weeks for the first opening with a counselor. Mark is thinking about changing his major, but is unsure of what he wants to pursue. At his first appointment, the counselor gathers information about Mark on an intake questionnaire and has Mark complete an interest inventory. Mark will be able to get the results of the inventory in two weeks. Mark is anxious about his career decision and needs to make a choice before registration begins in a few weeks. He hopes that the results of the inventory help him in his decision-making, but wishes that he didn't have to wait.

Jane is trying to choose a major and goes to the career center's Web site to find out what services they provide. She learns that she can receive career counseling over the telephone and is thrilled since she lives 60 miles from campus. Jane is able to sign up for a telephone session with a counselor online. Before the meeting takes place, Jane is directed to fill out an online intake questionnaire and survey about herself and her expectations about the counseling. In addition, she fills out an online interest inventory. The results will be forwarded directly to the career counselor. When Jane is called for her telephone counseling session, the counselor has already reviewed her intake questionnaire and the results of her interest inventory. The counselor begins the counseling process with a great deal of information about Jane and finds that she can dive right in to help Jane deal with her indecision. Jane immediately receives counselor-assisted interpretation of her interest inventory results that are integrated with the additional insights the counselor acquired through examination of her questionnaire and survey information. Jane feels much better after the first session with the career counselor.

The scenarios of Mark and Jane illustrate how using the Internet for distance career assessment can be beneficial for the client. Deciding what types of clients to serve and what services to provide are critical considerations. However, when you decide to provide career counseling or coaching via a distance model, you also want to consider what kind of assessment information you need with respect to your clients and how to access that information. Most, if not all, counselors and coaches do some form of quantitative and qualitative assessment when working with a client. This intervention usually employs formal testing instruments in combination with open-ended questionnaires that seek "expressed" comments from the client. It is important to be aware of advantages and potential limitations and to determine how you might provide these services when you are working in the distance modality.

Advantages of Distance Career Assessment

As the Jane scenario depicts, distance career assessment has some advantages over traditional career assessment. Some of these advantages include: availability of career assessment to a variety of populations, flexibility and convenience for the counselor and client, accuracy and speed of scoring and receiving results, providing for standardized test orientation, and employing up-to-date assessment instruments.

The use of online career assessment allows for greater access for many populations. Distance learners at institutions deserve to have the same kinds of student services as on-site students. The very reasons why clients are seeking distance learning opportunities are the same reasons why these individuals may need and profit from distance counseling and distance career assessment. Distance students can be directed to an online assessment, and interpretation can subsequently be provided through telephone, e-mail, chat, or video conferencing.

Career services professionals often desire to maintain contact with alumni on a national and international level. One of the challenges facing career counselors in colleges and universities has always been how to respond to alumni requests for career assistance. Certainly, many alumni may need career assessment in addition to other services, and the ability to provide this service via distance helps to meet the challenges faced by campus career centers.

Distance Counseling and career assessment also allow counselors to reach clients they might not have been able to reach before. This wider reach includes clients who live in geographically remote areas and shy or reserved clients who would not typically seek face-to-face assistance. In addition, clients with disabilities that prevent them from traveling to an office would also benefit from the accessibility of career assessment and counseling services delivered by distance.

Providing career assessment online allows the client greater flexibility to choose when and where to take the assessment (Barak & Buchanan, 2004; Sampson, 2000). This logistical advantage makes the test-taking more convenient for clients and allows them greater personal comfort. The process is more convenient for the counselor because immediate and accurate results can be accessed electronically, and the counselor does not have to administer the assessment.

Furthermore, there is the possibility for standardized test orientation through a well-designed Web site, which can offer theory-based information so that the rationale for the assessment and its relationship to the counseling is understood by the client (Sampson, 2000). Lastly, online assessments are likely to be updated more frequently than paper versions, so that counselors can make sure that the most recent, updated version of any given test is given rather than an obsolete version (Barak & Buchanan, 2004).

Potential Limitations of Distance Career Assessment

While the advantages to distance career assessment make it alluring, it is important to be mindful of potential limitations to ensure that we are offering best practice and appropriate service to clients. Some of these limitations include verifying psychometric properties of online assessments, protecting the client's confidentiality throughout the test-taking and interpretation process, ensuring counselor interpretation for the best use of assessment results, and controlling the administration of the assessment.

There are many different assessment instruments that are utilized in the career counseling and coaching areas, and even more are offered online including clinical and personality inventories. A quick search of the Internet can identify an amazing number of sites that offer free or low-cost career assessments. How do you as a counselor choose the best ones? When evaluating an assessment to use face-to-face, counselors and coaches have test publisher catalogs with information about the reliability and validity of the instrument. Even when you know the instrument that you use face-to-face is reliable and valid, you cannot assume that the instrument is also valid and reliable when administered via the Internet. Oliver and Zack (1999) researched 24 no-cost career assessment Web sites and found significant limitations ranging from validity of results to overall effectiveness in the career assessment process. It is the responsibility of the practitioner to investigate the psychometric properties of an online assessment before using it with clients (Sampson & Lumsden, 2000). Many career assessments delivered on the Web have no information regarding the assessment's reliability and validity. Any instrument being used online must enjoy validity and reliability by either equivalency studies or on the merits of its own research for Internet use.

There are resources for practitioners to find such information. The following Web site contains a review of online career assessments: http://www.quintcareers.com/online_assessment_review.html. This Web site provides test reviews of the Mental Measurements Yearbook online: http://buros.unl.edu/buros/jsp/search.jsp. The American Psychological Association provides instruction on how to find information on tests: http://www.apa.org/science/faq-findtests.html.

Protecting the client's confidentiality is extremely important throughout the distance counseling or coaching process, including the administration and interpretation of online assessment. If you gather qualitative assessment information through an online intake process, it is imperative that you provide appropriate levels of security for the transmission of this information. When using an assessment delivered online, it is recommended that you acquire an understanding of how the provider of the assessment collects, transmits, and stores information about clients' results.

Clients can access online career assessments without ever talking with a career counselor or coach. While this may be convenient for the client, it also poses a risk in that the client may misinterpret the results without counselor/coach assistance. It is fairly common to hear, "The test told me to be a _____." Those in the career counseling and coaching fields know that the career assessment did not tell the client what occupation to choose; rather it offered suggestions for exploration based on the answers the client provided. Many clients may not fully understand the assessment's purpose and limitations if they do not have the opportunity to discuss the results with a qualified counselor or coach. In fact, a client may make a decision about a career path based on a misunderstanding of the assessment results. As stated so well by Reile and Harris-Bowlsbey (2000):

> It is inevitable that many will take assessment instruments on the Internet without counselor preparation or intervention of any kind. Dependent on the nature of the instrument (Is it designed as a self-help instrument?), the quality of the instructions that surround the instrument and its interpretation, and the maturity of the client, this may be helpful to the client. To the extent that any of those components are flawed, assessment without the support of a counselor may do harm. (p. 79)

A major difference between traditional face-to-face assessment and distance assessment is the lack of control over the client's environment while taking the assessment instrument (Sampson & Lumsden, 2000). Some assessments are designed to be taken under certain conditions; and at the very least, we would hope that the assessment was completed while the client was in private, quiet surroundings. One approach to manage this challenge is to instruct clients to complete the assessment under appropriate conditions, or to ask them about the circumstances under which they completed it in order to be sure that the process was not compromised (Barak & Buchanan, 2004).

ReadyMinds Model of Distance Career Assessment

When career assessment is incorporated into the counseling process, as shown in the scenario of Jane, there can be many advantages. The ReadyMinds model, as discussed specifically in Chapter Two, demonstrates a successful example of how career assessment can be integrated within the intake process. Once clients have signed up for services, they fill out a General Survey (qualitative assessment), which provides the counselor with insight into their career and life planning situations and their expectations for counseling. These types of open-ended questionnaires can easily be administered via electronic means, and they provide an *expressed* assessment of the client.

The next step in the ReadyMinds Career Counseling process is for the client to fill out the Self-Directed Search (SDS), Internet version. The SDS is one of the most widely known and used instruments. An equivalency student comparing the Internet version of the SDS to the computer and paper and pencil versions found that the results of the Internet version were equivalent (Lumsden, Sampson, Reardon, Lenz, & Peterson, 2004). The designers of the ReadyMinds process ensured that the career assessment they were using was, in fact, equivalent to the other versions, so that counselors could feel confident that the results would be valid.

The results of this assessment are accessed by the counselor who is assigned to the client. The counselor can then interpret both the qualitative assessment information (General Survey) as well as the quantitative, *measured* assessment results (SDS) before meeting with the client via telecounseling. The counselor shares the results of the assessment with the client during the counseling process as is appropriate to each client's needs and situation.

ReadyMinds counselors also follow verbal protocols during their first session with the client. This semi-structured interview outline provides additional assessment information in the form of expressed responses. Furthermore, analysis of client experiences and behavior is also an effective assessment technique. Skilled counselors can analyze a client's experience via a resume or an open-ended questionnaire, and this behavioral record may enhance verbally supplied information about a client. This type of assessment focuses on the analysis of *manifest* or *experience-based* variables such as interests, skills, and values, but it also introduces many other useful client traits such as risk orientation, tolerance for ambiguity, intellectual curiosity, and motivational levels, to name a few.

The incorporation of varied types of assessment in the counseling process provides rich data for the counselor and, of course, the client. The counselor is able to get a broad picture of who the client is and what his/her needs entail. Incorporating assessment into the intake process also provides a way for the counselor to prepare thoroughly for the particular client's situation before the counseling process begins. This early access to information jumpstarts the counseling process and allows for counselor and client to begin from a point of mutual understanding. ReadyMinds counselors have found that this strategy often encourages clients to self-disclose important information. Clients have also reported that the very process of filling out a comprehensive qualitative questionnaire has sharpened their own awareness and insight with respect to important dynamics impacting their career decision-making. To further help clients understand all the assessment information, written summary documents are provided to the client upon termination. This carefully crafted communication allows the counselor to integrate multiple sources of assessment and provide results for the client in a way that supports the distance counseling process.

The ReadyMinds model is described as an example of how counselors can incorporate assessment into the distance counseling process. Each practitioner will need to examine how best to incorporate distance assessment into his or her services, scope of practice, and work setting.

Incorporating Distance Career Assessment into Your Distance Counseling Services

The National Career Development Association (1997)* has provided *NCDA Guidelines for the Use of the Internet for Provision of Career Information and Planning Services*. The section on Use of Assessment follows:

> If the career planning or career counseling service is to include online inventories or tests and their interpretation, the following conditions should apply:

*A revised version of these guidelines is expected to be released in mid-2007.

a. The assessments must have been tested in computer delivery mode to assure that their psychometric properties are the same in this mode of delivery as in print form; or the client must be informed that they have not yet been tested in this same mode of delivery.
b. The counselor must abide by the same ethical guidelines as if he or she were administering and interpreting these same inventories or tests in face-to-face mode and/or in print form.
c. Every effort must be exerted to protect the confidentiality of the user's results.
d. If there is any evidence that the client does not understand the results, as evidenced by e-mail or telephone interchanges, the counselor must refer the client to a qualified career counselor in his or her geographic area.
e. The assessments must have been validated for self-help use if no counseling support is provided, or that appropriate counseling intervention is provided before and after completion of the assessment resource if the resource has not been validated for self-help use.

It is important to be mindful of these guidelines and other recommendations in this chapter when incorporating distance career assessment into your services. Here are suggested steps you may take in order to incorporate distance career assessment:

Step 1. Determine what type of career assessment you will use in your distance counseling or coaching services and at what point in the counseling process you will use it.
Step 2. For assessment instruments, research the psychometric properties of the online versions of each instrument. Use the Web sites in this chapter, test publishers, and esteemed colleagues to find the instruments that will work best for you. Determine how confidentiality of administration and interpretation will be maintained.
Step 3. For qualitative assessment measures, determine how you will gather the information from the client in a secure manner. Adapt current questionnaires or develop new ones that will gather the information you need.
Step 4. Enlist colleagues and friends to test your assessment procedures.

*A revised version of these guidelines is expected to be released in mid-2007.

<u>Step 5</u>. Obtain feedback from clients regarding the assessment process. If there is evidence that a client does not understand the results, refer the client to a qualified career counselor in his or her geographic area. <u>Step 6</u>. Continue to monitor assessment procedures and make adjustments as necessary.

Counselor Tips for Taking Action

- *Make a thoughtful appraisal of each client's assessment needs and adapt both qualitative and quantitative instruments appropriately for distance use.*
- *Give careful consideration to each client's technical and verbal skills when making decisions with respect to the distance delivery of assessment.*
- *Explain to clients the advantages, challenges, and rationale for the role of assessment within the counseling process, and be careful to provide clear instructions regarding orientation and administration of such intervention on a well-designed Web site or by other means that are appropriate to the distance process.*
- *Pay particular attention to the psychometric properties of any instruments you plan to use in distance counseling to ensure that they employ the same degree of validity, reliability, and related characteristics that are required in face-to-face counseling situations.*
- *Ensure that clients who engage in distance assessment do so in environmental conditions that will not compromise their privacy or the accuracy of the assessment process.*
- *Gather appropriate pre-counseling information about clients when offering distance services so that you may integrate this data with additional insights you gain from actual counseling contact and quantitative assessment.*
- *Provide necessary security measures to ensure privacy and confidentiality when collecting, transmitting, or storing client assessment during the distance assessment process.*
- *Provide assistance with interpretation of distance delivered assessment unless the instrument is designed for self-help. Even in this case, many clients profit from additional interpretive help from the counselor.*

Questions for Chapter Review

1. What are the advantages to distance career assessment?
2. What are some potential limitations to distance career assessment?
3. Name some specific populations who could benefit from distance career assessment.
4. What are the advantages to incorporating distance assessment into the intake process?
5. What steps will you take to incorporate distance career assessment into your distance counseling or coaching services?

References

American Psychological Association. (2005). *Testing and assessment.* Retrieved June 26, 2005, from http://www.apa.org/science/faq-findtests.html.

Barak, A., & Buchanan, T. (2004). Internet-based psychological testing and assessment. In R. Kraus, J. Zack, & G. Stricker (Eds.), Online counseling: A handbook for mental health professionals (pp. 217–239). Boston: Elsevier Academic Press.

Buros Institute of Mental Measurements. (2005). Test reviews online. Retrieved June 26, 2005, from http://buros.unl.edu/buros/jsp/search.jsp.

Lumsden, J. A., Sampson, J. P., Jr., Reardon, R. C., Lenz, J. G., & Peterson, G. W. (2004). A comparison study of the paper-and-pencil, personal computer, and Internet versions of Holland's Self-Directed Search. *Measurement and Evaluation in Counseling & Development,* 37(2), 85-94.

National Career Development Association. (1997). *NCDA guidelines for the use of the Internet in the provision of career information and planning services.* Retrieved June 26, 2005, from http://www.ncda.org/about/polnet.html.

Oliver, L. W., & Zack, J. S. (1999). Career assessment on the Internet: An exploratory study. *Journal of Career Assessment,* 7(4), 323-356.

Quintessential Careers. (2005). *Online career assessment tools review.* Retrieved June 26, 2005, from http://www.quintcareers.com/online_assessment_review.html

Reile, D. M., & Harris-Bowlsbey, J. (2000). Using the Internet in career planning and assessment. *Journal of Career Assessment,* 8(1), 69-84.

Sampson, J. P., Jr. (2000). Using the Internet to enhance testing in counseling. *Journal of Counseling and Development, 78,* 348-356.

Sampson, J. P., Jr., & Lumsden, J. A. (2000). Ethical issues in the design and use of Internet-based career assessment. *Journal of Career Assessment, 8*(1), 21-35.

Support for Learning. (2005). *Jobsearch/assessment.* Retrieved June 26, 2005, from http://www.support4learning.org.uk/jobsearch/assess.htm.

CHAPTER SIX

How to Organize and Launch a Distance Counseling Program

Michelle Relyea

This chapter presents the experience of a former director of a career services office at a large university who has seen distance career counseling emerge not only as a benefit for the students, but also for the office and the university as well. The need for Distance Counseling in an academic setting is discussed; and the advantages it presents to students and the university are described through detailed examples of Distance Counseling programs.

The world of work has changed. The world of the nine-to-five workday is ever-changing. How individuals seek employment is itself a work in progress. "How has it changed?" you may ask. The Internet! With more access to information, the way we all approach our daily lives has undergone a revolution. Having worked in an academic setting for many years, I have seen radical alterations in the way students "learn." Therefore, it is important for student services on college campuses to address the rapidly developing needs of its student population.

Career Services Issues

For many universities and colleges, career services offices are staffed with low numbers of career counselors; yet, there are thousands of students filling classrooms each day. Most career offices provide access to counselors in the traditional 35-40 hour work week, some even providing minimal evening hours to accommodate working students. However, in most schools, the ratio of counselor to student is very high. At the university where I served as director (student population 8,000), there was one career counselor for every 1,300 students. Is it really possible to service the student body with low staff numbers? Absolutely not! Additionally, we only stayed open until 6:30 p.m. two nights a week to accommodate our evening student population. With most classes beginning at 6:00 p.m., students had 30 minutes to schedule appointments with their counselor. Although my university doesn't have a distance learning population, for the many colleges and universities that do, the career counseling offices never have contact with this ever-growing population of students. Furthermore, the alumni population usually receives very limited assistance due to the lack of adequate time and staffing.

University Issues

What is the importance of career services within the university/college mission overall? With placement rates becoming more and more important to attract students to college, career services must be a priority. However, on a college campus, it becomes very clear that everything is a priority. Each student service office is provided a budget, but salary line budgets are generally not very large. With the average salary of career counselors being 35K and benefits being 31% of that salary, it costs the university approximately 46K for an entry-level career counselor. Additionally, on some campuses, space becomes a factor. At my university, which is located in the New York metropolitan area, office space was an important issue to consider when hiring staff and adding new programs. Finally, in today's college marketplace, schools must consider the ever-growing distance population, the evening/weekend student population, and their need to access information 24 hours a day 7 days a week.

Throughout the last ten years, most schools have become completely online accessible. Students are able to register for classes, pay their bill, check financial aid, receive online tutoring, and access final grades, all online. Hence, student services have become online user-friendly as well. Without online services for students, a school is definitely limited in what it provides to the student population.

Student Issues

For many college students, academics are only one part of their daily lives. Some students have a full- or part-time job as well. Family and personal commitments often take time away from the focus on college education. College students at many universities have changed as well; for some universities, 23 years old is the average age of their students. With the growing non-traditional population of students and the variety of their outside commitments, more of these students are opting for distance education. More students are attending college after having gained work experiences. Some students have families. Therefore, flexibility of class schedules and services becomes very important to them. It is vitally important for colleges and universities to establish themselves as "easily accessible" by giving students convenient opportunities for the services they need.

Student issues often mirror departmental issues. If there are not enough counselors for each student to be seen regularly, the students do not have access to a career counselor on a regular basis. In some schools, career counselors are so booked up with appointments that many students never meet with a counselor. Finally, many colleges offering online distance education do not have accompanying online student services that meet the needs of this student population. Even if they do, many services are still provided during the regular working hours. The ReadyMinds Distance Career Counseling Program was designed to meet these challenges that career services offices, universities, and students face. At ReadyMinds, convenient and accessible career counseling is the foundation. The needs of the client are priority number one.

From my perspective as a former career services director, it was very clear that the information the counselors received before even meeting with the client helped counselors tremendously in understanding the overall background of the students they were going to be working with. It is almost impossible in a college career center to gain that much information before a student sees you. Additionally, with limited hours within the work day, it would take numerous sessions to gain the type of intake information provided by the pre-counseling strategies practiced within the ReadyMinds Program.

The quality career counseling that students receive from the ReadyMinds Program is never compromised. In most college career centers, the counselors are often playing a variety of different roles and wearing many hats during each day and academic year. Career centers are responsible to provide career-related workshops, on-campus recruitment days/weeks, annual or even semi-annual career fairs, and classroom presentations in addition to their day-to-day services. Considering all of the other aspects of a career counselor's position, counseling may often take a secondary role at various times throughout the year. Distance career counselors are providing only career counseling; hence, 100% of their time is focused on the client and the client's individual needs.

A professional and ethical distance career counseling program should be designed to address many of the students' needs with regard to scheduling, time constraints, online learning, and the changing world of work. At ReadyMinds, students have access to the program and counselor at their convenience. Evening and weekend students routinely "log-on," complete the necessary forms, and receive an e-mail from a counselor within 72 hours. The students have the opportunity to select counseling times that fit in with their schedules, whether these schedules revolve around work, classes, family obligations, or leisure activities. No traditional career center can accommodate students with such flexibility. Additionally, students are assigned to a counselor with expertise in their areas of interest. Again, this type of counselor/client "matching" is difficult to attain in the traditional career center.

A distance career counseling program addresses the university's career program needs as well. Providing online services does the following for universities: limits costs for a staff line; provides more counseling hours for students; addresses office/space needs; and services the distance/online student population. The costs for a distance career counselor will vary depending on what type of option is chosen. However, whatever the option, the costs are drastically different from hiring a full-time counselor. Consider the comprehensive costs of hiring and maintaining a career counselor: 35K (low spectrum); benefits (31%–including vacation time, sick time, disability, retirement accounts, and maternity leave, if appropriate); office space; and a computer station, phone, and office supplies. The average full-time employed counselor can cost close to 50K yearly (not including annual increases). Considering the option of hiring a part-time career counselor (who works 100% on career counseling activities), there are no benefit costs, no vacation or sick time, no retirement costs, no space/equipment/supply costs. At my university, the cost for the ReadyMinds Program and the part-time counselor to administer the distance program is close to 50% of the costs associated with a full-time employee.

Through the distance counseling program, the university offers online career counseling services that meet the needs of commuter, evening, and weekend students. Additionally, it can provide services to many of the underserved populations including alumni and continuing studies students. The online service, as it is developed for each individual institution, can provide a variety of different option times, including evenings, weekends, and lunch hours.

From a global perspective, universities are competing for students more than ever via open access to distance-supported education and services. Therefore, universities need to offer many different options to be as competitive as possible.

Setting Up Your Distance Counseling Program

Setting up a distance counseling program at your school takes some careful thinking and planning. First, keep an open mind. Traditionally, counseling has always been provided face-to-face. A distance counseling program may happen over the phone or via e-mail; therefore, it is important to think outside the traditional box. Having considered this new approach to counseling, do research of the Distance Counseling model. Once you have done thorough research, consider your school and its commitment to career counseling, placement, and technology. Additionally, as you begin considering any changes to your career services department, you must first complete a needs assessment. What are the strengths/limitations in the department/university? What are the populations the department intends to serve? What, if any, populations of students are not being serviced by your department? How many students are turned away each year due to an understaffed office? Is your career counseling staff too small, overworked, or underutilized? What resources can the department access to make changes? Most importantly, what is your long-term vision for your department? After considering these important questions and opting to have a Distance Counseling program, you can consider the following as professional research or actual working options:

OPTION 1: *Co-Branding or Private Labeling the ReadyMinds Program*

Realizing the time and budgetary constraints involved with providing counseling for all segments, the ReadyMinds Program, training opportunities, and consultant services can effectively assist your department in reaching specific populations of your choice in need of career counseling. This partnership can be created as a *co-branded relationship* or in a *private-labeled* manner with the "look and feel" of your own institution's offerings.

- Co-branded – The ReadyMinds service is positioned to act as an extension of your existing career counseling program and/or department. ReadyMinds will work with you to design, build, and maintain a Web page on your site that will provide access to the ReadyMinds Program. This portal will be co-branded and "powered by ReadyMinds." (View examples of two co-branded schools: http://oncampus.richmond.edu/academics/scs/career/ http://www.umuc.edu/careercenter/stu_counseling.html.)

- Private Labeled – ReadyMinds will work with you to design, develop, and integrate computer programming into your institution's Web site and the ReadyMinds Web site in order to customize the distance career counseling program with the "look and feel" of your institution. The client participating in the program will not know of ReadyMinds, since the service will appear to be an extension of your offerings (View an example of a private labeled school: https://secure.career.ucla.edu/alumlink/.)

OPTION 2: A Part-Time Distance Career Counselor Position

If budgetary restrictions are an issue, your institution could entertain hiring a *Part-Time Certified Distance Career Counselor to deliver the ReadyMinds Distance Career Counseling Program.* The package includes: a General Survey Intake form, the Self-Directed Search® assessment tool, 60 minutes of telephone counseling supported by online interaction, and a personalized summary report and action plan inclusive of appropriate resources to complement the career center's job search resources. ReadyMinds will also provide marketing assistance and will be liable for its services. The entire cost structure would vary depending on the contractual number of individuals your institution would like to service under this model.

- **The cost breakdown would be as follows:**

  - *X Amount (per annum) p/t ReadyMinds Counselor* - working from a remote office providing the counseling service to 100 - 500 individuals (depending on how many you contract for). You may target specific populations(s) such as current student population, graduate students, continuing ed., and alumni, as appropriate. You may interview and meet with the designated RM Counselor in person or via the telephone. The RM Counselor would, in a sense, become part of your payroll without the added expense of having to provide benefits, supervision, and additional space.

- *X Amount (per annum depending on the number of individuals contracted to be serviced) for the ReadyMinds Package* including all technology/web set-up and support, online products, supervision, telephone charges, customer service and resources.

OPTION 3: ReadyMinds Distance Credentialed Counselor (DCC™) Training Workshop

This training and credential are potentially of great benefit to counselors in a wide range of settings including colleges and universities, community colleges, high schools, professional associations, distance learning organizations, employee assistance programs, human resources, counseling centers, and private practice. The DCC™ Training sets the standard for excellence in this evolving practice specialty. Using this option, institutions can:

Send a staff member(s) to a DCC Training or participate in an online DCF™ Training.

or

Conduct a private DCC training.

Would you like to train and certify your entire staff or have several staff members gathered together from different institutions in your area? ReadyMinds will be glad to conduct a private training if a minimum of 25 participants are in attendance.

To learn more about the Professional Development and Training areas, please visit http://www.readyminds.com/dcc or http://www.cce-global.org.

Once you choose the option that best fits your school, consider a three to five year commitment to the Distance Counseling program. The first year will consist of marketing the Distance Counseling program. Using all of the resources available to you, consider which population of students would benefit most from a distance model. Plan a marketing strategy that will attract a number of those students. Include faculty support, your school's Web site, mailing campaigns, and advertising in the student center/student union. The best form of marketing will be student-to-student. Therefore, make certain the student population you first market to will be those students who will "talk" about the program. Here are a few comments from our students that I would like to share with you:

- "Please continue to motivate and encourage students, and graduates, to pursue our dreams and careers."

- "My counselor was available during hours that suit my busy life. My counselor was very understanding and I got a strong feeling from her that she really was interested in helping me pursue my objectives."

- "I was pleasantly surprised with the one-to-one personal relationship with the counselor, her effective communication skills and, above all, she maintained and displayed an empathic approach in several conversations. She is a superb and fabulous individual! I must admit I was skeptical about the program; after the conversation with my counselor, I realized the quality of the ReadyMinds Program is efficient and well organized. You deliver a high quality and professional staff that meets a standard of excellence within the realm of counseling sessions."

- "My counselor was very helpful. I can access the information online so I didn't have to take notes during our session."

Since establishing the ReadyMinds Program in our career office, we have increased the number of students who use the Distance Counseling program each year. The feedback from the students has been positive, and we have used the program to attract alumni support for our office. We have made a minimum five-year commitment to the ReadyMinds Program. Interestingly, the ReadyMinds Program at my school has sparked much interest in other types of online-based initiatives, including admissions programs and tutoring programs.

Whether you choose to consult with ReadyMinds, adapt their programs, or choose another type of Distance Counseling program, your career office will be "cutting-edge," providing a professional, ethical, useful, and much needed career counseling program for students. The many benefits, which include increased retention rates, will satisfy your office, your school, and, most importantly, your students. It is a win-win-win situation for all.

Counselor Tips for Taking Action

- *Address the rapidly developing and widely changing needs of your student population in light of evolving societal and demographic developments, including trends in technology.*
- *When designing delivery models for career counseling and related services, keep in mind pragmatic realities such as student-counselor ratio, students' schedules, and the needs of alumni.*
- *Acknowledge that the career and personal adjustment needs of distance learners are equal to those of traditional on-campus students; therefore, accessible counseling services of equal quality should be designed and delivered via appropriate distance models.*
- *Work with administrators to design and deliver counseling services via distance programs that employ appropriately chosen business models such as co-branding, private labeling, or a part-time distance counselor.*
- *Seek the appropriate training and credentialing such as the Distance Credentialed Counselor (DCC) Training offered through the Center For Credentialing in Education (CCE).*

Questions for Chapter Review

1) What benefits can be gained by analyzing your department's resources, budgets, and needs?
2) In evaluating a distance program, what are the objectives you intend to achieve?
3) Is it cost-efficient to implement a Distance Counseling option at your institution?
4) Should Distance Counseling training and research become part of overall professional development within your department?
5) How will you benefit from learning, researching, and adapting a distance program?

CHAPTER SEVEN

A Step-by-Step Approach for Adopting and Using Distance Counseling as a Private Practitioner

Denise E. Saunders

This chapter outlines a step-by-step approach for planning and adopting Distance Counseling services in a private practice setting. Areas of the planning and implementation process are discussed, including planning for Distance Counseling services, the logistics and set-up of a Distance Counseling practice, and implementing enhanced or new services to clients. The needs of the practitioner and clients are addressed to aid in decision making regarding distance modalities and ways to put them into practice. Issues and concerns unique to private practitioners offering Distance Counseling services to their clientele are highlighted.

The following narrative outlines how a private practitioner approaches the many challenges involved in becoming a Distance Counselor.

Sharon Brown, a private practitioner and Licensed Professional Counselor in her state, has been very interested in learning more about Distance Counseling. She was encouraged by advertisements for Distance Counseling training in professional counseling newsletters and excited to hear about this growing area of counseling from colleagues. Feeling strongly about the impact of technology on her own work, she began immersing herself in the literature. Sharon participated in Distance Counseling training to enhance her knowledge and skills and assist her in determining which distance modalities would best meet her clients' needs. Sharon was pleased to read in the pre-training materials that technology serves as a tool for use in counseling and does not become the counseling. She was further reassured by these words at the training. Her knowledge base and confidence in using distance modalities have grown significantly. However, she is uncertain where to begin or how to take the next steps.

Sharon's situation is not unlike that of many other counselors who have pursued training, reading, and investigation into Distance Counseling. It would be helpful to Sharon to identify the steps she needs to take in order to implement the use of distance counseling in her own practice. This chapter provides a step-by-step approach, which Sharon and other counselors and professionals in the coaching community may follow after deciding to use Distance Counseling methods with clients.

Planning for Distance Counseling Services to Clients

Deciding Which Clients to Serve

Perhaps a good first step in the planning process is to determine who you want to offer Distance Counseling services to. If you are a private practitioner accustomed to meeting face-to-face with a particular population or clientele, you may want to market your distance services to this same population. It makes sense to consider expanding one's practice by offering distance counseling services to current clientele because this is a population you are comfortable working with and you already have expertise in dealing with issues related to their specific needs. You may find that your clients can be better served via distance modalities due to concerns regarding travel or geographic location, discomfort meeting with a counselor face-to-face, medical issues or physical disabilities, which make it challenging for clients to come to an office for a counseling session. Clients have frequently sought out counselors with appropriate expertise who do not live in their immediate vicinity. As a result, they often have to travel some distance to meet in the counselor's office.

If services are to be offered to persons with disabilities, it will be important to assess the need for adaptive technology equipment and consider the unique requirements of this population. Clients with diverse ethnic or cultural backgrounds may also have unique needs. Distance Counselors must provide screening for suitability as well as appropriate adaptations of counseling communications and practices. Many private practitioners provide counseling or coaching services to organizations, which provide a rich opportunity for distance delivery. If geographical location and related travel are issues, one may want to seriously consider such options.

Counselors and coaches in private practice settings often have fewer resources and less support when they engage in Distance Counseling. Being aware of this reality helps counselors to anticipate certain challenges such as those surrounding the choice and use of various technologies. Depending upon your comfort and knowledge base regarding technology, a consultation could be sought to address particular issues to assist with the selection of technology and/or the most secure and effective platforms chosen for use in distance counseling. Being self-employed and working independently, however, does have its advantages. You can determine with a considerable degree of autonomy which distance methods to engage in and which clients you want to work with. This freedom may render the actual implementation process less cumbersome.

Screening Clients for Appropriateness of Service

Thorough and careful screening of clients for distance services ensures that each client's needs are best met and that counseling modalities are a good fit for the client and the client's presenting concerns. Not all clients will be comfortable working via distance. They may need some explanation with respect to how and why Distance Counseling services are being offered. As the professional providing the service, a careful determination of what you have to offer clients will make if far easier to decide which clients are appropriate for your services. At times, clients may present with issues beyond the scope of practice that is being offered. If this is the case, a referral to a qualified counselor would be appropriate. To illustrate an example, let's refer to Sharon and her practice:

> *Sharon received an e-mail from Elisabeth, a 36 year old, Caucasian female, who is going through a divorce. She has two children and is the primary caregiver. Given her current situation, she has decided that she must return to the work force after having been a stay-at-home mom for 10 years. In her initial message, Elisabeth expressed a desire to engage in career counseling to obtain assistance in making a decision regarding her career path. She found Sharon's name in the phone book ad which included her e-mail address. Sharon primarily sees clients with career concerns and markets her services as such.*

> *Upon further inquiry and information gathered from an initial questionnaire, Sharon learns that Elisabeth has been sleeping a lot,*

doesn't have much of an appetite, has lost weight, is sad and tearful, has been experiencing difficulty concentrating, and is quick tempered with her children. She denies having a plan or intent to hurt herself but acknowledges that she has felt hopeless about her situation for the past week or more. Elisabeth also shared that she had an episode of depression two years ago when she and her husband were having some marital difficulties. At that time she received counseling and began taking medication. Knowing Elisabeth's history and current concerns, Sharon decides to refer Elisabeth to another provider in the community who can assist her in dealing with the depression. Sharon encourages Elisabeth to contact her after seeking help for her depression when she will be able to make better use of the career counseling.

Sufficient intake information answers many upfront questions for the counselor and also informs the decision regarding client suitability for distance services. The intake information may take the form of quantitative data through the use of an assessment tool or it could be more qualitative in nature providing information about background and history, presenting concerns, and expectations of the work of counseling. Carefully crafting an initial questionnaire for clients to complete, which includes alternative contact information, will help determine if a client is appropriate for your Distance Counseling services. It will also provide you with a wealth of information about the client that will help to "jumpstart" the counseling process. At ReadyMinds, we have found that having thorough client information before engaging in the actual counseling helps to structure the exploration and goal setting process. This information can also be used to formulate hypotheses about the trajectory of the counseling sessions.

Deciding What Services to Provide

There are several options available to counselors who want to enhance or begin using Distance Counseling modalities in their practices. An important question to ask focuses on counseling environments: whether you are more comfortable working in a synchronous environment (communication occurring at the same time, i.e., telecounseling, chat, or video conferencing) or in an asynchronous situation (there is a lapse of time between communications, i.e., e-mail, listservs). Not everyone has a preference. Some counseling and coaching professionals will choose to utilize both synchronous and asynchronous methods of communication with clients including several different modalities, and others will choose only one modality, selecting something more familiar such as synchronous telecounseling. Regardless, identifying what modalities you intend to use for Distance Counseling will be critical in the planning stage. It is often the case that counselors discover during the training process that they have already been engaging in more Distance Counseling than they were aware of via the phone or through the use of e-mail to communicate with clients. Many have identified video conferencing technology as most closely emulating a face-to-face counseling session (Simpson, 2003). Continuing advances in this particular technology will assuredly afford counselors and clients increased opportunities for user-friendly counseling communication.

Distance Counseling serves as a frequent adjunct to face-to-face services in private practice settings, providing a way to augment or enhance current service delivery methods. Perhaps there are situations in which the professional is out of town and wants to be available to clients from a distance. Similarly, clients who travel or move out of the area may want to continue in a counseling relationship with the same provider despite the distance. In either case, Distance Counseling and coaching modalities allow for this flexibility and are often desired by the client. An alternative to using Distance Counseling as an adjunct to face-to-face is to market one's services for distance services exclusively. This service model allows clients to engage exclusively in distance services with the counselor.

Defining Counselor Availability to Clients

Setting limits and boundaries with clients can be challenging at times in face-to-face work. The issues become even more salient in different forms of Distance Counseling. How frequently is it assumed that, because the communication is taking place via distance (as in the case of Internet use), the response and or service should occur more quickly? It is important to establish comfortable limits as the professional aids in eliminating misunderstandings or miscommunication about when and how frequently the client can expect a response. Whether clients are communicating an inquiry about counseling services or as a function of the counseling relationship, boundaries regarding your availability to respond are appropriate and valid. No one person can be available to clients at all times, continuously providing high quality service in a face-to-face capacity or via distance. If e-mail is to be used as a form of Distance Counseling or as a mechanism to initiate contact, it would be helpful for the counselor to establish a timeline for a response. Typical response time for e-mail is approximately 24-48 hours. However, individual providers must determine what timeline is best suited to their practice and availability.

Additionally, professionals must consider whether they will provide short-term, problem focused counseling or guidance services or ongoing counseling with no predetermined limits. This decision is also dependent on individual counselors or coaches and the nature of services they wish to provide. Evaluation of distance career counseling using the ReadyMinds model (telecounseling with supported e-mail) suggests that a time limited model enhances the motivation of the client to do the work of counseling and assists the counselor in focusing on the goals of counseling (Djadali & Malone, 2003). Should a decision be made to offer more open ended counseling services, it is recommended that an agreed upon contract of service be established that would be re-evaluated at specified times throughout the counseling process (Rosenfield, 2003).

The Logistics and Set-Up of a Distance Counseling Practice

Maintaining Confidentiality

Clearly, the issue of confidentiality is a significant concern of practitioners and clients who are using distance methods. As ethical providers of counseling and coaching services, measures to ensure confidentially with clients, regardless of the delivery method, are paramount. There are several options to consider when ensuring that your communications via the Internet and/or the phone are confidential. Land based phone lines tend to be more secure forms of communication than wireless or cell phone technology. One innocent or accidental listening in of a neighbor's phone conversation on your child's walkie talkie will prove this point. It is the duty of professional counselors or coaches to inform and educate their clients about the limits of confidentiality using less secure phone lines. Due to the continuing explosion of technology options and calling plans being offered today, a growing number of individuals simply do not own landline or even cordless telephones. Since an alternative to the use of cell or wireless phones may not always be an option, sharing with clients the potential limits to confidentiality when using a cell phone allows them to make an informed choice.

Similarly, the Internet is an unsecured form of communication unless using software that encrypts messages to clients. As a private practitioner, this is an important issue to consider as you probably do not have the luxury of enjoying privacy protection from a larger organizational Internet service provider. Encryption scrambles the text so that, if intercepted in transit, it cannot be deciphered. It can only be unscrambled by the recipient who has a "key" to unscramble the text message. In order to ensure confidential communication via e-mail or chat, the use of encryption is required. Encryption software can be purchased by an individual provider from companies such as Pretty Good Protection (http://www.pgp.com). An alternative to managing and maintaining the encryption individually is to utilize a web based counseling platform that provides access to secure communication with several distance modality options. "Let's Talk Counseling" (http://www.letstalkcounseling.com) is one such Web site. Another is "Ask the Internet Therapist" (http://www.asktheinternettherapist.com).

With any form of Distance Counseling, every effort should be made to maintain confidentiality of client information. Thus, assessment information (either qualitative or quantitative), intake information provided by the client, and any form of counseling communication including records or notes of counseling contacts should be securely maintained. It is important to keep in mind, however, that just as 100% confidentiality can not be ensured in face-to-face counseling, so too it is impossible to make such a claim when using a form of Distance Counseling. Engaging in best practices in this area with a strong awareness of the issues will help ensure that you are creating the most secure environment for counseling communication to occur. Technology advances quickly. Keeping abreast of technological advances and their impact on counseling practices will assist practitioners in utilizing the most effective technology available to maintain client confidentiality.

Obtaining Informed Consent

Just as you would obtain informed consent in a face-to-face counseling relationship with a client, you must apply the same care when the counseling takes place using a Distance Counseling modality. Informed consent is obtained at the outset of the counseling relationship. Chechele and Stofle (2003) offer a list of "housekeeping issues" for informed consent that include: client awareness of differences in Distance Counseling and traditional face-to-face counseling as well as alternatives to Distance

Distance Counseling

Counseling, an understanding of where the counseling is taking place, the limits of confidentiality, and other related ethical/legal issues. Additional information regarding the fee structure, emergency contact and procedures, termination policies, and intake information procedures might also be included in the informed consent for clients to read and agree to before beginning counseling. These "ground rules" may be best presented in a written document that the client must either sign or agree to prior to engaging in the counseling relationship. Thorough, clear, and specific information to inform clients about your counseling practice or coaching services is essential.

Identifying Technology Needs and Technical Support

The technology needs of individual providers will be determined by the Distance Counseling modalities chosen for distance service delivery. If engaging in communication with clients (i.e., e-mail, chat, video conferencing), ensuring that you have both the hardware and software to do so in an ethical and efficient manner will be crucial to the design of your programs and or counseling services. Simple alterations to existing software such as making a switch to a high speed Internet service provider can significantly enhance counseling service delivery. Some distance modalities may require that you are using a high speed connection. Should video conferencing be a modality that will be offered, be aware that your clients must also have access to video conferencing technology in order to view the counselor during the counseling session.

If you are uncertain about what equipment to purchase or how to maintain privacy and security in your counseling communications with clients, you may want to seek consultative services or assistance from a technology expert. This support may be something that is established as an on-going relationship or merely as assistance in the initial set-up of your Distance Counseling practice. Staying current on available technology and its uses in Distance Counseling will help to ensure that you are using the most effective means to provide the best services possible for your clients.

Observing Legal and Ethical Issues for Private Practitioners

Ethical and legal issues are often of high priority when considering enhancing or beginning Distance Counseling. Private practitioners who are licensed in a particular state or territory are bound by the legal regulations of that license. The ethical guidelines by which you will practice as a professional counselor or coach are determined by both the professional organizations of which you are a member and also the certification or license that you hold. Legal and regulatory issues are perhaps the most challenging as there is continued ambiguity in this area. It is advised that counselors consult with their own state licensure boards regarding scope of practice guidelines and issues of regulatory control. Regardless of professional background and credentials, it is strongly recommended that private practitioners obtain liability insurance coverage. Professional counseling organizations such as the National Board for Certified Counselors and the American Counseling Association have information available regarding the purchase of professional liability insurance. Coverage for practitioners engaging in both full-time and part-time counseling services is available.

Koocher and Morray (2000) recommend the following regarding Distance Counseling:

- Counselors should assess their competence to deliver Distance Counseling services.
- Practitioners should receive confirmation of coverage from their insurance carriers (ideally written).
- Emergency practices should be planned and discussed with clients in the informed consent.
- Clients should be provided a statement of the limits of confidentiality to be included in the informed consent.
- Counselors should provide their clients with a detailed description of the services as well as terms and conditions (this may be incorporated into the informed consent).

Engaging in ethical practice with an awareness of existing guidelines, which strive for a "best practice" model of Distance Counseling service, ensures that, as professionals forging new territory, you move forward cautiously with an understanding of how these issues will impact your practice. Ethical and legal issues are addressed more specifically in Chapter Eleven of this book.

Distance Counseling

Establishing a Workspace

Deciding upon services to provide may assist in determining where your workspace will be. If you have access to an office outside of the home and it is conducive to Distance Counseling, you may consider establishing phone and Internet access in that setting to allow for communication with clients. Many providers engaging in Distance Counseling prefer the flexibility and low overhead (not having to pay for office space) of providing such services from a home based office. An issue to consider if you plan to provide services in an office setting outside the home would be whether you also have access to the Internet to communicate with clients between sessions or after hours. If establishing a work setting in the home, will you be able to ensure privacy and quiet while engaging in Distance Counseling? How best can you minimize the possibility of interruption?

ReadyMinds counselors conduct Distance Counseling primarily from their home offices and have found that this logistical arrangement works well. Keep in mind that there are numerous distractions to consider. Distractions at home include pets, other family members, phones ringing, call waiting or faxes being set (potential distractions if engaging in telecounseling), and the possibility that another person would be seen on screen by the client if someone entered the room while conducting a counseling session using video technology. Wherever you setup a workspace, accessibility to appropriate technology, the ability to secure client records and notes, dual calling capacity, and a quiet, private space in which to work with clients are a necessity.

Creating a Web Site

Numerous private practitioners and coaches have found the Internet to be a useful tool in communicating information to prospective clients. A simple Google search using terms such as "online counseling," "cybercounseling," "distance counseling," or "Internet counseling" will yield results demonstrating how many practitioners are providing services using the Internet. The content of these sites may help to determine how you choose to design your own Web site. Look for examples of well designed sites that provide information about specific services, fee structure, benefits, and limitations of Distance Counseling, links to various resource materials on the Internet, emergency referral procedures, and recommendations and further descriptions of the nature of Distance Counseling. Investigate several Web sites to compare information and determine what fees are appropriate for services you wish to offer. eTherapyweb.com (http://etherapyweb.com), has a useful breakdown description of fee structures comparing Distance Counseling services on the Internet including costs to the provider as compared to costs associated with face-to-face counseling services. As identified in Chapter Two, the ReadyMinds site provides clear, concrete information for prospective clients allowing them to make informed decisions about the career counseling services available, and thereby selecting service options that best meet their needs.

Implementing Distance Counseling Programs and Services

Pilot Testing Distance Services

Before offering services to paying clients, it may be helpful to pilot test your services. At a minimum, it would be good to have several individuals read over your Web site materials, or engage in communication using the distance technology that will be utilized. Consider obtaining a few clients who would be willing to receive services for no fee with the understanding that they serve as test cases. This strategy will help to reduce potential problems in the future and create a solid learning environment for the counselor who has engaged in minimal Distance Counseling work. There may be new or revised questionnaires that will be in place or new assessment tools which again need to be "tested" prior to offering them to clients. At ReadyMinds, we have found this preparation to be extremely beneficial in establishing our counseling program, and we continue to use a test case in on-going counselor training.

Marketing Distance Counseling Services

Planning for Distance Counseling can take time. Yet thoughtful consideration of the issues involved in the planning process results in a quality counseling service to clients. Now that you have determined the clients who will be served and what services will be offered, you are ready to market your service. A well-designed and informative Web site can be a useful marketing tool and should be considered as such when creating it. Other marketing options include brochures for use with clients and/or other professionals, directory listings, and phone listings in the yellow pages and other phone subscribers. Networking with other professionals and "spreading the word" that you are now providing these options will further market your Distance Counseling services.

Providing Supervision and Consultation

One of the challenges of being in private practice is the absence of peer support and consultation that is often available in other more institutional work settings. It is simply good practice to engage in supervision or consultation when offering new counseling services. Counselors offering Distance Counseling services for the first time will find it helpful to establish contacts for supervision or consultation to support their counseling work with clients. If possible, consider asking another counselor who provides Distance Counseling to serve as a supervisor as you begin developing skill in offering these services to your own clientele. Identify a counselor with whom you have a professional relationship and who is comfortable serving as a consultant, should you have questions or concerns that come up in your work with clients. For those who are engaging in private practice currently, a peer supervision or consultation group may already exist. The International Society for Mental Health Online is a wonderful support network for practitioners providing online services. Through their Web site (http://www.ismho.org), members have access to forums and listserv discussions regarding Distance Counseling practices. Securing sufficient support and supervision for yourself as you engage in new counseling modalities can ease the transition and provide mechanisms for feedback about skill development and effectiveness of services.

Establishing Professional Identity as a Distance Counselor

Until recently there were few resources available to assist counselors in establishing credibility as Distance Counselors. As Internet counseling services to clients with career and mental health issues have grown, more opportunities exist. The International Society for Mental Health Online has established guidelines for providers. Directories or web listings of online providers are readily available. You may choose to be included in one of these directories to gain recognition as a practitioner providing online services. Perhaps most significant of recent events is the Distance

Credentialed Counselor training provided by ReadyMinds that leads to the Distance Credentialed Counselor (DCC) credential offered through the Center for Credentialing and Education (CCE). For more information about the DCC credential see http://www.readyminds.com/training/overview.html Additionally, involvement in discussion groups and forums on Distance Counseling within professional counseling organizations can further develop a sense of identify and professionalism as a Distance Counselor.

Evaluating Distance Counseling Services

A brief mention of the importance of evaluating new services is warranted, although this issue is addressed more fully in Chapter Twelve. Program and service delivery evaluation is necessary to ensure quality services that result in counseling effectiveness. Distance Counseling services can be evaluated conveniently by using surveys or requesting feedback from clients less formally during the counseling process or after the counseling relationship has been terminated. In assessing the satisfaction and effectiveness of Distance Counseling services, a logical option is to request that clients complete an online survey. There are numerous Web sites that provide template models and generate reports of the evaluative data collected. One such Web site, SurveyMonkey (http://www.surveymonkey.com), allows for custom development of a survey designed specifically to meet the individual needs of the practitioner. This Web site has links to other related sites for comparison of web-based survey options. Whether the evaluative information is obtained formally through a survey or informally via the counseling process, it is helpful in evaluating satisfaction with the service and benefit to the client. Changes and adaptations can be made based on the feedback, resulting in enhanced counseling services.

Counselor Tips for Taking Action

- *Design a comprehensive plan that outlines the adaptations to private practice that are necessary for successful delivery of distance counseling services as either an enhancement of face-to-face work with clients or as the sole communication model.*
- *Give careful consideration to client suitability and establish a reliable method of screening individuals for distance services.*
- *Determine which specific distance modalities you will employ when delivering your services, e.g., telecounseling, e-mail, chat, or videoconferencing.*

- *Establish a protocol for explaining distance services to your clients and make sure that clients understand important issues such as maintaining contact between sessions, potential misunderstanding/technical problems, and referral procedures when necessary.*
- *Ensure that you and your clients address security and confidentiality measures in the context of the technologies you are using to communicate.*
- *Create clear and appropriate print/Internet-related information and marketing materials in order to ensure that your clients, potential or actual, understand the terms and conditions, including fee structure, of your Distance Counseling contract.*
- *Provide your clients with access to appropriate information regarding ethical, legal, and regulatory issues, including rights of redress, and adhere to the standards and guidelines that govern your scope of practice.*
- *Create a secure and private workspace that is appropriate to the delivery of distance services.*
- *As a beginning distance counselor, engage in "pilot-practice" delivery of distance services with appropriate partners in order to build your skills before the actual delivery of services to clients.*
- *Seek peer and association affiliation in order to establish professional identity and acquire a support system, including supervision, when delivering distance service.*
- *Seek evaluative feedback from clients in order to measure the success and effectiveness of the services you deliver via distance models.*

Questions for Chapter Review

1. How can counselors or coaches adapt current practices to include Distance Counseling services to clients? What important issues will need to be addressed?
2. How can I engage in Distance Counseling services as a private practitioner ensuring confidentiality for my clients?
3. What information will I seek from clients on an intake or initial questionnaire?
4. What resources can I utilize to develop a fee structure for distance services offered?

5. How shall I design a Web site that clearly communicates services offered and effectively informs clients of the benefits and limitations of Distance Counseling services?
6. How will I find supervision and consultation for Distance Counseling work with clients?
7. What resources are available to foster professional identity as a Distance Counselor or coach?

References

Chechele, P., & Stofle, G. (2003). Individual therapy online via e-mail and internet relay chat. In S. Goss & K. Anthony (Eds.), *Technology in counseling and psychotherapy: A practitioner's guide* (pp.39-58). New York: Palgrave MacMillan.

Djadali, Y., & Malone, J. (2003). Distance career counseling: A technology-assisted model for delivering career counseling services. In G. Walz & C. Kirkman (Eds.), *CyberBytes: Highlighting compelling issues of technology in counseling* (pp. 7-16). Greensboro, NC: CAPS Publications.

Koocher, G., & Morray, E. (2000). Regulation of telepsychology: A survey of state attorneys general. *Professional Psychology: Research & Practice, 31*, 503-508.

Rosenfield, M. (2003). Telephone counseling and psychotherapy in practice. In S. Goss & K. Anthony (Eds.), *Technology in counseling and psychotherapy: A practictioner's guide* (pp. 93-108). New York: Palgrave MacMillan.

Simpson, S. (2003). Video counseling and psychotherapy in practice. In S. Goss & K. Anthony (Eds.), *Technology in counseling and psychotherapy: A practitioner's guide* (pp. 109-128). New York: Palgrave MacMillan.

CHAPTER EIGHT

Distance Counseling in Action

Karen Ricci

This chapter illustrates Distance Counseling in action within a variety of settings. It provides specific, concrete examples of Distance Counseling communications including online assessments, chat samples and telecounseling transcripts. High school career/college planning with students and parents is covered, as well as career counseling in community colleges, four year institutions, and government agencies. Using the ReadyMinds model, we will cover the spectrum of career planning communication techniques from assessment to exploration, decision making, and job search. This approach provides a very practical, hands-on review with creative and experience-based applications of theory to actual practice.

As time goes on and generations evolve, the one sure thing about life as we know it is that change will occur. As we look at serving the "Generation Y" population, also called the Millennial Generation, the Net Generation, or even, "NeXters" (Wikipedia, 2005), it is more important than ever to adopt new techniques and technology to serve them effectively. The Net Generation includes people born between 1979 and 1994 in the United States. Their numbers total some 60 million people.

This generation has grown up with home computers, music downloads, instant messaging, and cell phones. They tend to be highly pressured to succeed and have had many aspects of their lives programmed for them by parents and schools. They are the most watched and most tolerant generation in history. The expectations and methods of this generation differ greatly from their predecessors, "Generation X" (Zemke, 2001).

The "Gen X" generation constitutes a mere 18 million folks, all born in the mid 1960s through the 1970s. This was the first generation to survive a hurried childhood of divorce, space shuttle explosions, and open classrooms. This generation saw a rise in SAT scores—yet heard themselves denounced as so wild and stupid as to put "The Nation at Risk." In jobs, they're delighted to take risks and prefer free agency to corporate loyalty. Sometimes criticized as "slackers," they nevertheless were widely credited with a new growth of entrepreneurship and the resulting "dot com" boom.

So you can see, for almost 80 million people in the United States, aged 18 to 40-something, the means and methods of communication and their missions and values have changed radically from the "Boomer" generation (Hill, 1996). It makes perfect sense to explore and develop methods and strategies for counseling practices that suit the needs and expectations of these very populous generations.

The way we work affects the ways we live, and this is true also for counseling. People are more mobile, more stretched for time, and are accustomed to having information at their fingertips – when and where they want it. Telecounseling, asynchronous chat, webcams, and many combinations of these techniques are the ways of the future. ReadyMinds has developed a variety of techniques and strategies to address how the changes in our world have impacted the delivery of counseling services.

As a career counselor, I've had the opportunity to work with a wide variety of populations over the years, from high schoolers to career changers. I've worked with men and women from a very wide variety of cultural and educational backgrounds and from a broad range of geographical locations. I've learned a lot about the similarities and the differences that one may discover among a very motivated population of career seekers.

One of the things I've noticed repeatedly about populations in North America is that people are often identified by their career label. This phenomenon cuts across many generations and includes both males and females. When we put a lot of value on labels, criteria such as interests, values, personality, and abilities are often given less weight than they deserve within a careful career decision-making process. Happily, the trend toward finding one's "passion" in meaningful work has made its way to the forefront in recent years (Bolles & Figler, 1999). The merging of these two trends, greater technological literacy and seeking more intrinsically satisfying work, influences our journey to review Distance Counseling in action.

Let's begin by reviewing what kinds of counseling I'm talking about. Many counselors have adopted means and methods to provide Distance Counseling for different kinds of concerns ranging from career counseling to psychotherapy. My experience lies entirely with career counseling, and that is what I will report on.

There are many similarities between Distance Counseling and face-to-face counseling. Most importantly, the theoretical bases are not unlike. Most of the skills and techniques that counselors learn in graduate school for traditional counseling are also used in the Distance Counseling model. As Bolles and Figler reported in *The Career Counselor's Handbook* (1999), there are seven basic subjects that career counselors focus on: job development, job assessment, job hunt counseling, career development, career assessment, career planning /career counseling and lifework planning. Within the ReadyMinds model, Distance Counselors cover each of these areas, and more.

Differences between Distance Counseling and face-to-face counseling can prove to be significant (Goss & Anthony, 2003). Most importantly, the distance model is much more accessible to people than the more traditional model. Many people have no idea of how to access a career counselor or don't have local access because of geography, transportation issues, time issues, and so on. Distance Counseling opens up the service to many who would otherwise go unserved (Bloom & Walz, 2004). Another important difference in the Distance Counseling model is that it can be done at more convenient times for clients. Think of busy college students racing from class to work with little time to spend on planning or exploring their future. With the Distance Counseling model, these students can log on to their computers or arrange convenient telephone appointments outside of the typical 9-5 time slots and obtain information, guidance, and counseling from a trained professional. Anonymity is a factor that I had not really given a lot of credence to before becoming a Distance Counselor; but I'm finding that many clients will open up much more quickly to me using telecounseling or asynchronous chat than they would in face-to-face counseling. Finally, Distance Counseling provides clients the ability to proceed at their own pace, in their own way, affording time for thoughtful reflection and processing of information. It also provides a written record for the client to refer back to for clarification or confirmation.

Distance Counseling

My overall impression of Distance Counseling has been very positive. It is a very satisfying professional experience to write about the work I have done with distance clients in order to demonstrate its effectiveness with various populations.

First, let's take the case of a high school student. The needs and concerns of the North American high school student revolve primarily around deciding "the next step." In our cultures, graduating from high school is indeed a "mark in time," or a very significant transition from childhood to adulthood. The needs in terms of counseling at this stage of development tend to include information gathering and career awareness after engaging in appropriate introspection in order to understand one's motivations, desires, interests, values, and personality traits. The developmental span is very wide for this population, with some students being very capable and ready for self-awareness and life planning, while others are less focused and less able to grasp these more mature concepts. Nonetheless, the role of the career counselor at the high school is to prepare the student for the "next step." Understandably, the challenges for providing these services in a meaningful, relevant fashion are huge.

One solution for meeting the needs of the more motivated student is to provide an in-depth program through the Distance Counseling model. I would like to recount the case of "Nancy" for you in order to demonstrate the process.

> Nancy is a very competent senior in high school with high aspirations and many plans for her future. While she has had some exposure to career exploration on her own and through her classes, she is hungry for a more personalized career counseling experience. Having Nancy fill out a detailed general survey outlining her ambitions, goals, and questions proves to be a very helpful tool for both Nancy and myself. Answering very specific questions forces Nancy to organize her thoughts in a way she has not experienced before. Taking the SDS (Self-Directed Search) assessment online provides even more insight into the nature of Nancy's interests and personality, especially as they relate to the world of work.
>
> Following Nancy's initial survey and assessment, I have the luxury of going over this material at my convenience. I am able to check out her

high school on the Internet (most high schools have Web sites now), so that I have an idea of what her community is like, what the expectations of the students in this community are, and even the name of their football team! I prepare and send a welcome e-mail to her explaining who I am and what she should expect from our counseling sessions. I am able to approach my first session with Nancy with much more information than I would likely have with any new "traditional" client. What's even more valuable, I am able to formulate questions before our meeting to encourage Nancy and to put her at ease.

At an agreed upon time and date (done over the Internet via e-mail), I place a call to Nancy to "continue" our counseling relationship. It's always pleasurable to "meet" a client for a conversation, feeling like I already have some ideas of what the needs are and how I might best approach them. I believe the client is generally more at ease as well, from the brief e-mails we've already exchanged and my welcome message to her.

At this point, I am able to use most of my traditional counseling skills, with the exception of interpreting body language. However, what I have discovered is that my listening skills have greatly intensified. Pauses, hesitations, and remarks I might not have focused on in a face-to-face session suddenly have more impact and significance. I really enjoy the fact that, as my client and I have our conversations, I am free to take notes and focus on her words, inflection, and omissions, and I find myself prompting her with vocalizations rather than eye contact. My client is also free to get comfortable, lying on the bed or floor or wherever she might be located in her private setting. She doesn't need to worry about what to wear, whether she's had a chance to shower after soccer practice, or any of the other roadblocks that might pose problems for some students.

Following our initial conversation, we would typically arrange for a second conversation – usually of a somewhat shorter duration. For most high school students, the one hour telephone counseling in combination with e-mails seems to be sufficient to help them advance in their career planning. When our telecounseling is complete, I write a summary of all we've discussed, including information and resources for further exploration. I believe that this format for Distance Counseling is extremely effective for high school students, given the fact that most high school counseling offices are understaffed and overbooked. Many high school students are "hungry" for the attention and information they receive during our Distance Counseling sessions. This personal attention and encouragement can make the difference between whether a student elects to pursue higher education or not – an important consideration given the most recent labor market surveys for the future.

In addition to providing counseling and information for career planning, the Distance Counseling method provides very concrete information on what the "next steps" are. By developing a timeline with the student, strategies are accurate and informed. Parents appreciate this very detailed information as well, especially as it relates to financial planning for the future of their student.

A less motivated high school student can also find value in the Distance Counseling methods. I've had several less than enthusiastic young adults who have been sort of pushed into counseling by frustrated parents. I find that, generally, I also have very good results with these students. While some students may act uninterested and uninvolved, the truth is that most are very anxious, even frightened, of "the next step." Students often report that they feel out of control and pushed into decisions that may be confusing to them.

The anonymity of Distance Counseling is often a welcome relief to the pressures and expectations students often impose on themselves at this stage of their lives. I find that high school students can be very frank and forthcoming with a Distance Counselor, venting, discussing, and exploring in their own way, at their own pace. The power of the written word and the attentive tone of counselor communication are valuable resources. In moments of doubt, students may access them and find support.

Included in the Distance Counseling model is the concept of self exploration. Web sites are offered and referred to on a regular basis and can even by referenced during a conversation. This type of synchronous, technology-supported communication comes naturally to this young generation.

Distance Counseling for the community college student has also been very effective. Many of the same issues and concerns exist as with the high school student, but there seems to be more urgency to many of these clients' concerns. The community college student comes in three main varieties:

the student who intends to transfer to a four-year college; the student who is more vocationally-oriented and interested in a shorter term educational experience; and the student who is very definitely "lost." Community college students constitute a large and varied population, ranging from young, high school graduates to job-changers, re-entry women, and those who are continuing their education by necessity, upgrading skills for current employment. Often, community college students are the most time-stressed group of individuals; for many are trying to balance work, families, and school all at once. Distance Counseling can prove to be just the right resource for already jammed schedules!

Let's review the case of "Jose", a young man of twenty-two who, by his own admission, feels to be at a "crossroads" in his life.

Jose is currently attending community college sporadically. For the past three years, he has signed up for classes each semester with the best of intentions and then finds he has to drop classes due to time/financial restrictions.

Jose's responses to the general survey are very brief. His answers tend to be short and don't display much insight about himself for me to "get to know" him. When asked about his strongest interests (activities enjoyed), his response is "to pay the rent and make his car payment." In the next question about his strongest skills, he reports that he is a hard worker who goes to work everyday, even when he's feeling ill.

Jose doesn't have a clue about what he wants to do in life; he's on what I call "survival" mode. When I review his online SDS (Self-Directed Search) assessment, I discover that he is Realistic (R), Investigative (I), and Artistic (A). The SDS has given me a wealth of information prior to our beginning the formal counseling process.

Because Jose has chosen a counseling plan that involves only online communications, I have a wonderful opportunity to formulate some very pointed questions to "fill in the blanks" on Jose's general survey. Since Jose's work hours aren't consistent, the asynchronous chat model for career counseling is a great match for him. Here is a sample of what I posted on Jose's personal page, along with the results of his SDS and that report:

On your General Survey, you indicated that you have tried to take a very active role in finding the "perfect" career, but that you often get "sidetracked" with more immediate needs. As you read your SDS results, pay close attention to your 3 highest "type area" scores: realistic, investigative and artistic. Be sure to review the job titles associated with your three highest types (RIA, RAI, IRA, ARI, AIR, IAR). Notice your very high preference for realistic. You appear to be a "hands on" type of person. Individuals with score patterns like yours tend to prefer to work with things, more than with people. They are usually described as being genuine, honest, practical, and goal-oriented. They generally like to be able to "get the job done," without a lot of discussion and collaboration. This SDS type description sounds quite similar to many of the qualities that you disclosed about yourself in your General Survey.

When Jose read his welcome message, he responded to my message with the following:

Thank you for your welcome letter. I have read the SDS report. I find much value in this report. I think I took it about 5 years ago and it didn't help me (maybe because I didn't get any counseling with it). I don't necessarily like all of the jobs the report offers, but at least I think I'm understanding myself a bit more. But I think I need someone who can work with me to help me make some decisions about which way I should go for my future. I feel I need to make a commitment to something and go for it.

As you can see, Jose is very interested in moving forward in this counseling process. The motivation and desire are apparent, and he appears to be developmentally ready to take on the challenge of deciding his "next steps." I will be able to use my traditional counseling skills and strategies to work with this client in a comfortable manner. I will definitely be aware of Jose's cultural priorities as I help to guide him through the process of not only choosing a career pathway, but also helping him understand the implications of his decisions. By giving Jose the information he needs to make informed choices, we can work together to create a very concrete document defining his "next steps." This will include a timeline for setting up exploration, decision making, education and training, financing of his studies, and expectations of jobs once the training is complete.

While this is a very comprehensive process, Jose was pleasantly surprised to learn that with the guidance he received, including the directed homework he did with Web sites and informational interviews, he was able to have a concrete plan in place in less than a month. He didn't have to miss work or school to meet with me, and he was able to be honest and frank in his e-mail discussions because he didn't have to face me. He was very motivated to come to a decision and to have a plan in place since he wanted to become engaged to be married and needed to have reached closure on some important life decisions to feel secure in his role as a husband.

Working with students at four-year colleges and universities is also a challenging and rewarding experience. Having worked as a career counselor in a university setting, I am very aware of the difficulty on many campuses of getting an appointment with the career counselor due to busy student schedules, too many students, and too few counselors. The Distance Counseling model is one that, again, appears to be a perfect solution for busy students. One of the primary concerns for this population is which major to choose. Many students want to examine the connection between their college major and the "real world," particularly in terms of being able to find satisfying jobs once they graduate. These students have many ideas of what life will look like once they graduate; and I find that many students want confirmation that their ideas and ideals are, in fact, possible. I have also seen many students at the collegiate level who are truly in search of finding their passion. They are motivated to take control of their futures and to find careers that will add value to their lives, both personally and professionally. For this population, many options for counseling plans are available.

Let me review with you a client who chose a Distance Counseling plan that combines telecounseling and personal e-mails. Jana is a young lady with a very creative inclination. She has moved to New York City to begin her undergraduate education at one of the outstanding universities in the city. Here is her response to my welcome e-mail:

> *I think the SDS report was very accurate describing my RIA summary code. I have almost all of the qualities of the realistic, investigative, artistic, and conventional types. I'm not enterprising, but I do believe that I'm somewhat social. But, I wouldn't like helping other people with their problems, I'm not idealistic, patient, or overly friendly. As far as*

the list of occupations go... I'm not in total agreement! I understand that these are just a few suggestions. It doesn't bother me that there are things listed on here that I would never consider! I thought it was kind of funny! I loved the list of hobbies the SDS provided, I'll be sure to try some of them out! And, thanks for the list of art centers you provided me, I'm going to take a class in pottery in January, and possibly basic drawing, woodworking, jewelry making, computer-aided art, and I'm going to attend lectures and seminars at various museums throughout the year! I found the SDS suggestions of how I can gain more insight into different careers and areas of interest very helpful, and the book list at the end is great too. I will definitely go to the library and check them out.

I'm the type of person that is going to switch careers many times in my life. It's just the type of person I am, and I'm fine with that. I want to study everything in college! I want to earn a double major, or a minor, so that I have a background in different things. I want to enjoy the experience of learning, and I'm so lucky to be in NYC to have this opportunity (even though I don't like the city that much, but I'm getting used to it). As for switching of the fashion merchandising major... I read a book after I enrolled in the major that described fashion merchandising. It was the most boring book ever! I know that I couldn't work at any job they described. I also worked at a retail store for a year while in high school, and my managers talked about their different jobs with a fashion merchandising degree, and they sounded horribly dull! I read descriptions of courses in the advertising major, and it sounds so interesting! But, I have this pre-conceived notion that advertising is immoral and all about money, and shoving products down peoples' throats. I think the fashion industry is kind of like that as well. Way too materialistic!! But, I'm sure it's not all like that. I don't want to pre-judge anything! The career center at my school is closed right now, but next week I'm going to make an appointment, because I have loads of questions to ask. I'm going to take you up on your idea begin writing a resume also. I might work on it with someone at school, but I might ask you for a few suggestions. I don't have any more questions right now, but when I do, I know where to find you! Thank you again for matching me up with those Web sites! It's really provided me with so many great opportunities! Talk to you later!

As you can see, this is an extremely bright, motivated student who really just needs someone to help her sort through the options available to her. Being able to give her very concrete information allows her to explore options and opportunities she had not considered. I very much enjoyed working with this client because she was so enthusiastic; and I believe she enjoyed the opportunity to "talk" to a counselor about the things she was feeling and realizing as she took classes in her major. As you've probably noticed, I do refer her to her school's career center and have given her the phone number and extensions she needs to set up an appointment. I don't want to replace the services her university offers, only to enhance them.

Finally, I am happy to share with you the fourth "population" I've had the pleasure of working with, the career changers. People change careers for a wide variety of reasons, from company downsizing to being replaced by technology. Some decide to change careers as their children grow up and become independent; and others decide to finally follow their passion. No matter what the reason, large portions of our society are involved in changing careers. This state of flux definitely has many ramifications for people. For some, there is an immediate need to become re-employed; for others, the journey can be leisurely. The truth of the matter is this – the Gen Nexters will be the largest population of career changers in all of history. These young people will change careers between five and nine times during their adult lifespan. These individuals will work for upwards of 50 years, and will not be retiring until they reach their seventies! The number of people we see changing careers right now is nothing compared to the changing that will be occurring in the next decade!

Let me share with you the case of a client who was very definitely filled with frustration and anxiety about his future. This client is in his mid-forties and has been unemployed for a few months. He has submitted resumes to everyone he can think of, but has not received any calls or interviews. We worked together on the phone and through e-mail over a period of several weeks. This is a portion of my summary to him.

> *It has been my pleasure to work with you in the ReadyMinds Program. Thank you for taking the time and effort to participate actively throughout our correspondence. Please consider this statement to you as a summary of the issues and questions we covered during our career planning communications.*

In my Welcome Message, I suggested to you that I found your Self-Directed Search scores relating to your stated interests in careers involving social services or business to be very accurate. At that time, I also pointed out your type preferences for social, conventional, and enterprising areas. As you know, your SDS report contains detailed definitions of these type preferences.

Jonathon, one area of concern that you expressed in your General Survey as well as in your questions and comments in the ReadyMinds Interactive Communications Area, dealt with career possibilities. You asked for my insight into fields that you should look into. I responded suggesting more research and the need for you to name your interests as well as your strongest skills. I provided Web sites that could assist you in this.

You mentioned in your General Survey that you were interested in several occupations in the education/social service area, which, of course, correspond very well to your stated interests in conflict resolution/arbitration. But you also mentioned at least a bit of interest in computer gaming and educational administration. You also mentioned on your survey that activities you enjoy a lot include being outdoors, traveling, and spending time with friends. While your Enterprising area (on your SDS career assessment) was your strongest, not far behind are your social and organizational interests. I think you are wise to do some informational interviewing, which is interviewing people who do some of the careers you are interested in. This is a very non-threatening interview for both you and the person you will talk to because you are not looking for a job, rather, just the individual's perspective on their chosen occupation.

Jonathon, I encourage you to refer back to our notes and conversations as you do your informational interviews. Please use the "contacts" you've mentioned to assist you in getting interviews with the people you really do want to speak with. Your background is rich and varied. There are many occupations that you are very well suited for; your task is to determine which is the best for you at this juncture in your life. Please don't hesitate to e-mail me with any questions or concerns which might arise as you move forward. Know that the list we've developed together is a very valuable tool – one that will guide you as you proceed. Know that the resumes we've worked on are excellent,

*and that your personal investigation of these chosen possibilities will
lead you to selecting which field is the best one for you now.*

As you can see, we've taken on huge topics of conversation – this man's
professional life and interests – and have been able to create some order in
the chaos. This gentleman learned a lot about his priorities and his passions
during the course of our "conversations"; and he was able to rediscover
what an amazing range of skills and talents he had acquired over his
professional life. He also learned how to "transfer" some of these skills to
other occupations, many that made him feel re-energized and excited about
the future. The counseling skills for this Distance Counseling are basically
the same as I would use in a face-to-face situation; but this client is able to
walk away from our meetings with a very concrete, written plan as to what
his "next steps" are to be. Again, with a relatively short amount of time for
counseling, this distance client was re-energized, armed with a new set of
career options and resources for reference and referral, and a very specific
plan, complete with resume, to "go out and conquer the world."

In summary, as you can see from the examples I've given, Distance
Counseling is a very effective tool. I feel I've given my clients a great
strategy to move forward in their lives. I know I've given them great
resources and references; and I believe that the benefits of Distance
Counseling are extremely tangible and verifiable. Distance Counseling
doesn't really involve huge changes in the way you assist clients. As I said
earlier, the underlying theoretical bases are the same as I use with my face-
to-face clients. However, delivering services to people in the best way
possible, at their convenience, without disrupting their busy lives, with
comfort and decreased anxiety, appears to be a very viable solution to the
problem of getting people to counseling.

From the counselor's standpoint, many of the same benefits are seen. I'm
able to schedule clients in the evening or early morning or on weekends
when I have time available. I'm able to take the time to investigate their
current situations, which may call for researching schools, cities, or career
fields, and to put together comprehensive reports and findings for them. I
enjoy the research and investigation – and I enjoy helping this wide variety
of individuals to find their passions.

Counselor Tips for Taking Action

- *Familiarize yourself with your target populations in terms of demographics and related technology-supported communication preferences.*
- *Give careful thought to the kinds of clients you will serve and the counseling services you will be delivering: mental health, career, educational, and possible therapeutic services.*
- *Master the various forms of Distance Counseling delivery that you will offer in your practice, such as written e-mails, telecounseling, chat, or computer-supported services.*

Questions for Chapter Review

1. How does the Distance Counselor evaluate the technology skills of potential clients to ensure their suitability to engage in Distance Counseling?
2. What are the best ways to adapt effective face-to-face counseling techniques for distance delivery in specific modalities of counseling such as mental health, career or therapy?
3. What kinds of intake information or assessment techniques are most effective for the Distance Counselor to employ as a means to evaluating the counseling needs of various client populations?
4. What specific adaptations does the Distance Counselor make when offering services via distance delivery modes such as telecounseling, e-mail or chat?

References

Bloom, J. W., & Walz, G. R. (Eds.). (2004). *Cybercounseling and cyberlearning: An encore.* Greensboro, NC: CAPS Press.

Bolles, R, & Figler, H. (1999). *The career counselor's handbook.* Berkeley, CA: Ten Speed Press.

Goss, S., & Anthony, K. (2003). *Technology in counseling and psychotherapy: A practitioner's guide.* Houndsmills, UK: Palgrave MacMillan.

Hill, R. B. (1996). *History of work ethic.* Retrieved April 4, 2004, from
    http://www.coe.uga.edu/workethic/hcontext.html

Holland, J. L., Powell, A., & Fritzsche, B. (1994). *SDS professional
    user's guide.* Odessa, FL: Psychological Assessment Resources, Inc.

National Board for Certified Counselors & The Center for Credentialing
    and Education. (2004). *The practice of internet counseling.* Retrieved
    July 26, 2005, from http://www.nbcc.org/webethics2

Wikipedia, The Free Encyclopedia. (n.d.). *Generation X.* Retrieved July
    26, 2005, from http://en.wikipedia.org/wiki/Generation_X

Zemke, Ron; (2001) *Generations at Work, Managing the Clash of the
    Veterans, Boomers, Xers and Nexters in Your Workplace.*
    Retrieved on April 12, 2004, from
    http://www.centeronline.org/knowledge/Article.cfm?ID=615&

CHAPTER NINE

The University College London (UCL)/ReadyMinds
Career Counseling Program: An International
Distance Counseling Partnership

Marco Federighi

This chapter describes the pilot collaboration between UCL Engineering and ReadyMinds and how this collaboration relates to the development and delivery of UCL teaching and learning strategies. It begins with a description of the background of the collaboration, followed by the feedback from students after the first two years of operation. The role that this collaboration is expected to play in UCL's international strategy is discussed. Additional topics include UCL's strategies for recruitment, professional accreditation, and services to alumni. The chapter concludes with an outline of some likely future developments.

Working with ReadyMinds

We were referred to ReadyMinds because of a series of fortuitous coincidences and for entirely different purposes; but after contact was made, we were impressed by the range of opportunities that collaboration between the University College London (UCL) and ReadyMinds could offer. Given our intention to link university study and post-university professional development with a strong emphasis on international careers, ReadyMinds appeared from the start to have a number of very attractive characteristics:

- It is a U.S. firm and can advise engineering students on the market that is potentially the most important one for them – the U.S. corporate market.
- It has a long track record of working with universities – we contacted a few of them, including Harvard, and were impressed with their feedback.

- It does most of its counseling by distance delivery, which is crucially important for our international students, particularly for their post-university professional development and for our activities with alumni.

Before exploring in greater detail the possibility of working with ReadyMinds, we carried out an analysis of the market for other possible partners, and we consulted our own Careers Service to assess their compatibility. On both counts, our conclusions were in favor of collaboration with ReadyMinds, especially because the combination of distance delivery and partnership with universities is highly unusual. As far as their compatibility with the UCL Careers Service was concerned, we decided to work with both in a complementary manner in order to avoid unnecessary overlap and duplication of effort. UCL Careers Service provides, as it always has, face-to-face advice to residential students and talks/seminars to students and staff about career opportunities, with a focus on the UK; ReadyMinds would provide Distance Counseling to our students on international exchanges, with a focus on the U.S. and, more generally, on international careers.

We were also kindly permitted by ReadyMinds to take part in their training program for Distance Counseling; and the experience reinforced our confidence in the method and in the company and provided us with valuable insights in a field in which we still had only limited experience.

Student Feedback

As a pilot for the UCL/ReadyMinds partnership, UCL students on the UCL/California Institute of Technology (CalTech) exchange were given bursaries for ReadyMinds counseling in 2003/04 and 2004/05. All students have provided feedback to both ReadyMinds and UCL; and their views have been considered by the Faculty Teaching Committee, which has decided to continue the pilot and, subject to the provision of additional funding, its gradual extension to our other exchanges with U.S. universities.

Student feedback has concentrated on three issues: the quality of the counseling provided by ReadyMinds; the pros and cons of Distance Counseling versus face-to-face counseling; and the role of career counseling in the UCL programs of study.

The quality of the ReadyMinds counseling has been praised by all students. Counselors have been seen to be helpful, knowledgeable, and supportive; and their advice on the writing of CVs and resumes has been particularly well received. The distance delivery method used by the counselors (telephone) has also been favorably rated and has not been regarded as inferior compared to the face-to-face counseling available at UCL. Comparisons with Web-based technology have been made, on the whole, with no specific recommendations about the relative merits of one or the other technology. Also, in terms of value for money and flexibility, the ReadyMinds service has attracted very favorable comments.

Somewhat surprisingly, all students have queried the relevance of career advice in their own individual circumstances, since all of them had already decided the immediate direction of their career development after the end of their studies at UCL. All students selected for the CalTech exchange were very technically focused, and their interest in a wider range of career opportunities was limited. Two of them said openly that they had not sought career advice from UCL (which is free), and would not have sought it from ReadyMinds if they had not been asked by us to do so! Maybe our best students have already made up their minds by the time they reach their third year. This degree of certainty with respect to career choice is not uncommon among technology-oriented individuals. If so, the specific career needs of internationally-focused services to high-ability students in engineering and technology fields may need to be re-examined. It may be that the services they require deal more with job search and employment seeking behaviors as opposed to introspective self-assessment and related exploration or decision-making.

On the whole, however, the UCL/ReadyMinds pilot has been a success, although its fullest benefits will not manifest themselves until the redesign of all our degree programs has been carried out. This task is expected to take at least another three to four years. The first programs will be rolled out by the Department of Civil and Environmental Engineering in 2006/07.

In the next few sections, we will discuss how the collaboration between UCL and ReadyMinds is linked to our teaching strategy and our international strategy, and how it contributes to the delivery of both.

International Issues

The UCL Faculty of Engineering Sciences is international in two respects (as far as students are concerned): we have a very high proportion of students from outside the UK (about 35%); and we have a number of student exchanges with universities outside the UK.

International exchanges have existed since the 70s and normally are part of 4-year MEng (Master of Engineering) programs in which the third or fourth year is spent at a foreign university. Participating universities vary from department to department, with some schemes extending to the whole engineering faculty and a few extending across the whole of UCL. The places available on each exchange are few, in some cases because funding is limited (for example, in the case of SOCRATES-funded exchanges within the European Union), in other cases because of the requirement of keeping each exchange financially neutral for the participating universities. For example, the exchange between UCL and the California Institute of Technology (CalTech) allows two UCL students each year to go to California for the whole academic year in exchange for five CalTech students coming to the UK for one semester. Students on exchanges are jointly supervised by a faculty member in the host university and a UCL faculty staff who keeps in touch as necessary by e-mail and telephone. Each student submits a study plan for approval by the Engineering Faculty Teaching Committee and is given credits that are equivalent to one full year at UCL. Giving so much weight for a year abroad is rather unusual, and this policy reflects the importance we attach to our undergraduate exchanges.

The 35% of our students who come from outside the UK are not with us on an exchange scheme, but are full-time students in our BEng or MEng programs (3 years or 4 years). Those from outside the European Union pay a higher fee than UK and EU students, who are partially subsidized by the UK government. They come from the Far East, Australasia, the Middle East, Africa, Europe, and the Americas. Upon graduation, some of them go back to their country of origin and start their careers there; some stay in the UK; and some move to a third country. Their careers often take them to two or three different countries, very often in careers outside their university specialization.

Our exchange schemes are financially neutral and require much more work from administrative and academic staff; but we value them for two reasons:

they offer our students the opportunity to experience first hand the teaching of engineering in a different country and culture, thus enhancing their employability in international careers; and they serve to stress, in the eyes of possible students, our credibility as an international university. In both respects, our exchange schemes greatly benefit from our collaboration with ReadyMinds, which, on one hand, will provide students with up-to-date, specific information about the most internationally important job market and, on the other hand, will further emphasize our international credentials and, more importantly, the link between our teaching and the careers of our graduates.

Exchanges with the most prestigious foreign universities, such as CalTech and Columbia, are routinely oversubscribed; and only the best students are allowed to go. We wish our international students to be ambassadors for UCL, and we select them on the basis of their wider range of interests and not only on the basis of their academic ability. Keeping numbers on exchange programs low helps to emphasize their character of highly selective programs, only for "high fliers." We pay the counseling fee for students in the ReadyMinds program in the form of a bursary (scholarship), which serves to reinforce the same message of an elite service for elite students.

Needless to say, the pastoral and academic care of students away from UCL is a major issue in the quality assurance of international programs. In this respect, too, the expertise of ReadyMinds in Distance Counseling is something that we regard as very valuable.

Recruitment Issues

The recruitment of students into engineering schools in the UK has been declining for years. This is normally attributed at least in part to an image problem, with engineering seen as "dirty" because it is linked to manufacturing and thus offering a less desirable career than law or medicine. This is normally held to be chiefly a UK problem; and a comparison is often made with supposedly more buoyant recruitment in the U.S. and in continental Europe, not to mention Japan and China.

The other reason for the declining interest in engineering is held to be the decreasing pool of suitably qualified school leavers, and, in particular, the decreasing number of school leavers with an A-level in mathematics. Again, this is normally portrayed as a mainly UK/English problem, partly due to the excessively specialized curriculum after the age of 16, which is very different from the broader curriculum in the U.S. and Europe.

This picture is only partly correct. Higher interest in engineering in other countries hides a worldwide inability on the part of engineering schools to attract the top 10% of the school leavers in terms of ability. This has been reported in Germany, France, the U.S., Japan, and China. The main reason cited is the same as in the UK, that is, the perception of engineering as linked to manufacturing and, therefore, as professionally lower than, say, law or medicine. Thus, not only does engineering have an image problem that is not limited to the UK, but the problem is not so much the numbers of students who want to study engineering, but their quality.

More interestingly, the conventional wisdom confuses two things that are different: engineering as a field of study at university and engineering as a career after university. This confusion is fostered by academics, who fail to point out to prospective students that engineering graduates have a far wider range of careers than any other graduates, including graduates in law and medicine. This happens for a variety of reasons, but an important component is simply the lack of awareness on the part of academics of what their graduates do in their careers.

Another interesting factor that is neglected by the conventional wisdom is that students do not shun all engineering schools and programs indiscriminately. In fact, sharp differences in the popularity of schools and programs exist in the UK as well as in other countries. The two main factors which appear to affect students' choices are the perceived prestige of a university (and thus of the degrees awarded by it) and the structure of the programs of study in engineering. This last point merits some comments, especially in light of the diminishing pool of students who appear to be suitably qualified for engineering studies.

Traditional applicants to engineering programs in the UK have three A-level passes in the sciences, usually a combination of three among Mathematics, Further Mathematics, Physics, Chemistry, and Biology. The pool of applicants with this kind of qualifications has been decreasing steadily for a number of years, with Mathematics being a reason of particular worry. This decrease is normally blamed for the decreasing trend in applications to engineering and science programs across the country.

Many engineering programs, however, are suitable for students with "mixed" A-levels, (i.e., two in the sciences and one in the humanities or, less frequently, one in the sciences and two in the humanities). However, students with this broader mix of qualifications only rarely study engineering. These students are interesting for two reasons: one, because they represent a significant fraction of the whole university population; two, because there is strong anecdotal evidence that they do better than their more "technically focused" colleagues after initial difficulties in their first year, and tend to have careers leading to higher and more influential positions.

We carried out an informal market research exercise among UCL students to find out more. We talked with more than 80 final year students from elsewhere at UCL, all of them with "mixed" humanities and sciences A-levels. Interestingly, the result of this limited, and certainly not very professional, investigation was in agreement with anecdotal evidence from the U.S., Europe, and China, suggesting that able students with a broader range of interests can only be interested in the study of engineering if, one, they are made aware at an early stage that studying *engineering opens up a very wide range of careers*, arguably more than any other field of study, and, two, engineering programs of study are focused less on educating future PhDs and researchers and more on *educating future business and industrial leaders*.

There is one main conclusion from this: faculty and staff must acquire a much greater understanding of what is required of engineering graduates outside research and academia in order to project to possible students the wide range of careers available to them and to design curricula that can educate them to a much less technically focused professional role.

In the case of UCL, there is a further aspect that deserves attention. As stated above, about 35% of engineering students at UCL are from outside Europe, with a further 7% from other European countries: all in all, just under half of our student population is from outside the UK. Most of these students, once they graduate, will work for large multinational companies in the U.S., Europe, and Asia, and will probably experience two or three significant career and country changes before they retire. Many of us believe that an emphasis on this international side of the careers of our graduates, together with the broader, career-oriented curriculum outlined earlier in this section, could be the key to attracting students in the elusive top 10% of the ability range.

Professional Accreditation, Continuous Professional Development, and Distance Delivery

A further aspect of our engineering programs merits consideration, and that is their accreditation by the professional institutions in engineering. The Engineering Council in the UK has recently developed a new framework for the accreditation of professional engineers, UK-SPEC (UK Standards for Professional Engineering Competencies). The first draft of the implementation of UK-SPEC by the IEE (Institution of Electronic Engineers) and by the IChemE (Institution of Chemical Engineers) lists five areas, one of which (Economic, Social, and Environmental Context) is entirely non-technical and another (Design) is also largely non-technical. Designing a curriculum of this kind will, however, require from faculty and staff a much greater awareness of what non-academic engineers actually do than they normally have. This will, we hope, attract more able students to the study of engineering (as discussed in the previous section), but will require on the part of curriculum developers a much greater awareness of what graduates in engineering will do in their careers, not only in the UK, but throughout the industrialized and the developing world. Here again, the involvement of ReadyMinds and the UCL Careers Service in complementary roles will play an important role.

The UK-SPEC accreditation framework identifies two criteria for the accreditation of an individual engineer: *competence* and *commitment*. The former is what a professional engineer can do *at the time of his/her accreditation* – technical skills, professional skills, and the knowledge underpinning them. The latter is the commitment to *lifelong professional development* – the updating of skills and knowledge as required by the practice of his/her profession. Traditionally, university programs have focused on *competence* and developed it in a short period of time, typically 3 or 4 years full-time and, for a minority of students, a few more years part-time. Post-degree professional development has been left to employers and professional organizations.

We believe that continuous professional development after university will be a very significant growth area for the providers of education, and we wish to take part in shaping it. For this, we will need to develop a wide range of short courses with a professional focus. Moreover, given the international character of our potential customers, we need those courses to be distance-delivered to them in their workplace, including the distance delivery of tutorial support, assessment, career planning advice, and professional mentoring. This leads neatly to what is perhaps the most promising aspect of our relationship with ReadyMind: the possibility of providing Distance Counseling and distance learning, integrated in a coherent program designed for our international graduates.

Distance delivery of degree programs, and of the support that goes with them, is not something that is new to us. One very successful example of distance delivery in engineering is the British Telecom Masters in Telecommunications Engineering, which has been developed by UCL for delivery to BT employees in the UK and to employees of an associate company in Mumbai and Poona (India). The course is delivered in collaboration with other universities and uses a variety of technologies for teaching, support, and assessment. This is, however, a degree-awarding program and not yet a Continuous Professional Development (CPD) program. It does show, however, how an international audience can be provided with advanced education and professional support which are entirely distance-delivered.

Alumni Issues

In general, European universities are less good at keeping in contact with their alumni than are American universities. We have decided to change this relationship and to create an alumni network, which, together with our partner universities abroad and with our partners in the professional and business sector, will support our programs of study in a number of ways:

a. By providing feedback on our programs of study and their effectiveness in preparing graduates for their careers.
b. By helping our fundraising campaigns.
c. By providing professional support, for example, with the recruitment and selection of students, with the international accreditation of our programs, and with the maintenance of our network of international partners.

By being part of our network, our alumni will be offered the possibility of continuous professional development (CPD) through a suite of programs consisting of short courses and interactive academic support. Since our alumni are working in more than 50 countries across the five continents, distance delivery will be the primary avenue for CPD provision. As discussed in the previous section, our own expertise in course delivery and ReadyMinds' expertise in Distance Counseling will both contribute to the interaction with our alumni in the same way as they will contribute to the interaction with our current students on international programs.

Future Prospects

Our collaboration with ReadyMinds is expected to develop in three directions: 1) the extension of their counseling to our students in all international programs; 2) the training of some of our academic staff in distance support for our students in distance-learning programs; and possibly 3) the delivery of career counseling to students in affiliate programs in other universities. We will now briefly discuss each point in turn.

The *extension of career counseling* by ReadyMinds to our students on international programs and/or to our international students depends on two things: increased funding and a better understanding of which students might benefit from it the most and be most interested in it. The two issues – of funding and scope – are related because UK/European students and non-European students are funded differently and are interested in different programs.

UK and EU students pay a much reduced tuition fee (with the difference being paid by the British Government) and their full living expenses, whereas non-EU students pay a full tuition fee as well as their living expenses. International programs appeal to both cohorts, especially programs with a stay in a U.S. university. However, *all* of our international programs are four-year "integrated" Masters (MEng), which are less interesting to non-UK than to UK students because the MEng qualification are less internationally recognized than the MSc. Furthermore, non-UK students are *already* abroad when studying at UCL, and many do not feel the need for one year somewhere else. As a result, international MEng programs tend to be taken more by UK students, whereas most non-UK students enroll in BEng programs (which last three years and have no provision for an international exchange) and then enroll in a one-year MSc.

This dichotomy means that most international students who are coming to UCL to open for themselves the possibility of an international career miss out on the U.S. connection of which ReadyMinds is a part. This could be remedied by opening up ReadyMinds counseling to all students, either by subsidizing it (as it happens now for students on international programs) or by simply advertising it as well as making it available (as it is already). Still, the full range of opportunities resulting from our links with U.S. universities will not be available to most students unless it is de-coupled from international exchange programs by providing links of a different type (e.g., visiting professors, summer schools, common projects carried out at a distance). These matters are currently under consideration and will probably be addressed in the framework of our re-designed programs which have been briefly discussed in the previous section.

Regarding the *training* of our staff, two issues must be addressed: one is their lack of awareness of what the careers of engineering graduates really are; the other is their lack of training for distance support and monitoring of international students. The first issue can be addressed by providing staff with suitable formation courses, giving a detailed overview of the international careers which are open to engineering graduates. This could be done by the UCL Careers Service and by ReadyMinds together, with focus on UK and U.S. careers respectively and could be supported with staff development funds.

Academics already provide support to students on exchanges by using a variety of methods, chiefly e-mail, but also phone and occasional face-to-face visits. However, this support is often sporadic and is always demand-led, with students providing the lead and academics giving their support reactively rather than proactively. To be sure, much support on campus is also demand-led, but residential students have the benefit of regularly scheduled face-to-face tutorials in small groups of five or six. This could be extended to students on exchanges by using existing technology (e-mail, phone, web-based chat rooms, bulletin boards); but academic staff are currently not trained to provide this kind of support in a structured manner. Again, this is an area where ReadyMinds and UCL could easily work together – with ReadyMinds providing expertise on distance support rather than on careers.

Finally, the *provision of teaching* to students in affiliate universities is something that many universities are considering. The University of Nottingham has recently opened a campus in China, and it is likely that its example will be followed by others. UCL is unlikely to follow this route, but we are considering the development of an International School of Engineering in China in collaboration with Chinese and U.S. universities, where the entire curriculum would be taught in English and monitored by the universities participating in the consortium. Clearly, this kind of venture would be facilitated by distance delivery of courses (e.g., from internationally renowned academics in the UK and the U.S.) and of support (e.g., to students on summer schools and semester-long or year-long visits). This would be even more critical for CPD courses for UCL alumni which could be distance-delivered to their places of work. Again, ReadyMinds could work with us in a dual capacity – to facilitate the distance delivery of support not specifically linked to career counseling and to provide career awareness via one-to-one counseling and distance-delivered courses to students in the affiliate campus. These matters are under consideration, and are likely to be developed within the next few years.

Summary

Universities are adapting to changes in their student populations and to a much more diversified and international job market for graduates. They are also competing increasingly to attract the best international students in a global market where both the student intake and the careers of graduates are increasingly international. A curriculum that leads to good international careers and accompanying individual career planning services are vital for the effectiveness and appeal of universities that wish to be global players.

The function of university career services is twofold: to advise individual students about the career choices open to them; and to provide academic departments with the career awareness they need to develop and improve their curricula. In the Faculty of Engineering Sciences at UCL, we are working with the professional institutions in engineering, with the UCL Career Service, and with ReadyMinds to bring career awareness to the heart of our teaching curriculum.

CHAPTER TEN

Challenges and Special Problems in Distance Counseling: How to Respond to Them

Heidi B. Ravis

This chapter examines various kinds of challenging situations that may arise during the practice of Distance Counseling. Some of these scenarios are specific to distance modalities, while others are variations of situations that also arise in face-to-face counseling practice. Counselors are offered suggestions and strategies for managing these challenges and minimizing the risks they may pose.

In 2001, I received a flyer in the mail from ReadyMinds, announcing an upcoming training for National Certified Counselors interested in delivering career counseling via distance. Intrigued, I submitted a resume and was subsequently invited to attend a 15-hour training program. At the time, I was working part-time in a private practice setting, providing clinical career counseling services. I was thinking about what else I might be able to do that would provide additional challenge, opportunity for professional growth, and, of course, income. Flexibility was key since my two children were young and I did not relish the thought of returning to full-time employment. The training sounded like an avenue worth exploring.

Now, several years later, I do the majority of my work via distance. In addition to counseling ReadyMinds clients and case managing approximately 15 counselors, I provide distance career counseling services to graduate students and alumni of a large urban university. My clients, colleagues, counselors, and supervisors are spread throughout the country and, in a few cases, have lived in other countries. I no longer do private practice work because I am too busy with my distance work. Although I travel to other parts of the United States to conduct Distance Credentialed Counselor (DCC) training workshops in person, my training partners live far from me. This means that our preparation for the workshops, including communication with the ReadyMinds corporate office, is conducted from a distance.

When I began my ReadyMinds journey, I had a number of concerns both about the efficacy of short-term Distance Counseling and my ability to deliver quality services to clients using this model. One of my primary concerns involved the use of technology. The counseling work itself would occur via telephone, which was not a problem, but written communication would take place largely using a secure Web supported platform. I would need to post documents to a client's page on the ReadyMinds site and follow posting procedures more complicated than cutting and pasting in order to do this. My own computer knowledge at the time was purely practical and utilitarian, and some of these procedures were foreign to me. My learning curve was steep, and I made frequent use of ReadyMinds tech support in the early days of my involvement with the company. Luckily, the office staff was extremely patient and encouraging. I was determined to master the skills I needed in order to deliver Distance Counseling.

Technology Factors

Counselors who are considering distance work in any modality need to assess their own level of comfort with technology. They will also need to make decisions about which forms of distance communication to use as they serve their clients. My ReadyMinds work, for example, involves telephone counseling with Internet support (i.e., e-mail, postings on an encrypted site, message board). Counselors may choose to begin with one method that feels most comfortable, and expand technology-supported practice options to other methods after appropriate training.

Similarly, counselors will need to assess the client's ability to use the technology necessary for the counseling relationship to take place. Suler et al. (2001) give a thorough outline of factors to assess in making these determinations, including the client's preferred method(s) of therapeutic contact and technical skills. If the initial contact from client to counselor is made online, it is likely that the client has some measure of comfort with this form of communication. If the client seeks the counselor out in person, however, the counselor will need to explain the options available and work towards a joint decision based on all the factors related to client suitability. Suler et al. give a thorough outline of factors to assess in making these determinations.

The majority of difficult situations, in my experience, arise from technology issues. E-mail messages may be lost or may not reach their intended recipients. In one instance, I sent several e-mails to a newly registered client and received no response. The client contacted the ReadyMinds office after realizing that the counselor was not receiving his responses to her e-mails. The office staff then had to serve as a "go-between" and route e-mails from the client to me. Fortunately, this solution facilitated communication between the two parties, and counseling was successfully conducted via telephone.

Technology may fail in more basic ways as well. Storms and power outages can wreak havoc with distance communication methods. Power failures can disrupt scheduled sessions. It is important to collect contact information from clients – and share counselor contact information with them – so that there are alternate means of reaching one another in such a situation. There are also reported cases of spontaneous and unanticipated noise intrusions, such as from construction crews or landscaping teams, that might appear suddenly and impose interference with telecounseling sessions.

I Can't See You!

An area of concern for most counselors considering Distance Counseling methods (with the exception of videoconferencing) is the lack of visual cues provided by counselor and client. While this does present a challenge, many Distance Counselors report that they are able to find ways to compensate for the absence of visual information. Rosenfield (2003) states, for example, that counselors offering telephone counseling services may learn to listen more intently and carefully, thereby gaining a great deal of information in this way. They may be more likely to attend to tone of voice, rate of speech, and use of language to deepen their understanding of the client. Chechele and Stofle (2003) point out that counselors using e-mail are advised to ask clarifying questions and closely examine the meaning of the client's communications. Writing style and use of language, punctuation, and symbols can give important clues about the client's personality and mood. In other words, it is not that cues about the client are lacking; it is more the case that these indicators are available in alternate forms.

It is crucial for the counselor to provide clear information to the client and to address any potential areas for misunderstanding. Over the telephone, counselors may find that they need to "check in" with clients more frequently by asking questions about their perceptions of the conversation. This may be especially true when there are periods of silence, which can feel particularly long in a telephone conversation. Making sure that the client understands what the counselor is saying and clarifying any information that may seem ambiguous can help to prevent miscommunication and advance the work of the counseling relationship.

Once they begin doing distance work, counselors may find that clients actually feel more comfortable revealing sensitive information via these methods than they do in face-to-face counseling. Several authors, including Suler (2001), have described the "online disinhibition effect," which refers to this phenomenon. Clients may find the lack of visual cues liberating, allowing them to disclose personal material without fear of judgment. Rosenfield (2003) suggests that this applies to telephone counseling as well. Research evaluations from ReadyMinds (Malone & Miller, 2002), as well as anecdotal reports from ReadyMinds counselors, indicate that counseling relationships can develop successfully without the visual information present in face-to-face counseling.

The Importance of Preparation and Support Structures

Three crucial components of any Distance Counseling program are support, structure, and supervision. These elements can help to reduce risk and facilitate resolution of difficult situations. A counselor working in isolation is more vulnerable than one working within an organization or institution, where there are likely to be systems in place to help resolve difficulties. Regardless of whether a counselor is working in a solo practice setting or as part of a larger organization, it is important to have a support system in operation before embarking on Distance Counseling. Taking time to do research, prepare a policy statement, and design a program can help to guide practice and minimize the potential for problems later on. Further, having colleagues available for support, guidance, and supervision can make the process less daunting and isolating.

It is also important to have clear upfront information and an informed consent form. Clearly stated policies that offer guidelines for communication between counselor and client can help to prevent or minimize misunderstandings and confusion. They should also outline the responsibilities of both parties. This information should be available on the counselor's (or organization's) Web site and/or provided to the client in hard copy form. These policies should be discussed with the client to ensure comprehension and reinforce the information.

Additional Considerations

Most difficulties I have encountered in my work with ReadyMinds have been commonplace and not unlike those that occur within face-to-face counseling situations. Sometimes clients register for services and then do not respond to communications from their assigned counselors. Other times, counselors contact clients at scheduled appointment times and the clients are not there. Fortunately, ReadyMinds has protocols for dealing with these situations, but tracking missing clients down can be frustrating and time-consuming for the counselor. It is important for counselors to recognize and address the impact of these inconveniences so that they do not contaminate their work with the client after re-establishing contact. Again, this points to the need for support and supervision in the counseling process so that the counselor has the opportunity to discuss these matters with someone familiar with Distance Counseling issues.

Identity verification and management provide another potential area of difficulty. On the one hand, many clients seeking distance services find the relative anonymity that it offers to be an appealing feature. Counselors must, however, be able to establish verifiable client identity and collect basic information about clients, at the very least for billing and emergency purposes. By employing appropriate security measures, counselors can protect client confidentiality and offer adequate safeguards to client information. These protections may help to allay any client concerns about their vulnerability in the counseling relationship.

Clearly, it is easier to *wear a mask* online. Goss and Anthony (2003) suggest that it can be useful to examine log-in names for subtle insights about a client. If client is a minor, there is a need to verify identity and get consent from a parent or legal guardian. Counselors may inform the minor that the counselor reserves the right to verify with a phone call the validity of required parent-sent e-mail permission. Obtaining a notarized signature from a parent is also an option. Considering the popularity of technology-supported communication among today's youth, we may anticipate that they will be a group that is open to distance services.

There are two distinct challenge levels to identity management. First, how to ensure at the beginning of the counseling relationship that clients indeed are who they say they are. Second, during the subsequent counseling contacts, how do counselors verify that they are dealing with that same individual? For the latter case, the use of a password or some personally identifying piece of information is helpful. Some Distance Counselors require photocopied driver's licenses (or related documents) before the counseling begins, especially when engaged in video-assisted counseling. Others insist on digital signatures or a faxed copy of a written "informed consent" document.

The first scenario is a more challenging one. The possibility of impersonation is always present. Additional verification strategies may range from insisting on an initial face-to-face session to establish client identity (not always possible) to requiring that the client confirm specific details of identity such as age, residence/phone number, student ID (if applicable), possible referral source, and any other information that would show a "good faith" effort on the counselor's part to authenticate accurate identity. What is important is to demonstrate reasonable, professional "due diligence" via this procedure as well as to have the client formally agree to honest self-representation as part of the registration process.

Security is another potential area of concern. Clients may share e-mail addresses with family members, or members of their own household or workplace may have access to their e-mail. Both counselor and client are advised to give serious consideration to security measures including password protection or encryption to minimize the risk of confidentiality violations. Counselors working via telephone are advised to convey to clients, in advance of the initial session, the importance of being in a quiet setting during telephone appointments. They should also explain the advantages of "land line" phones and potential security risks of cordless and cell phones. Despite clearly stated pre-counseling instructions on our Web site, ReadyMinds counselors have reported a few isolated instances when they called a client for a scheduled session, only to find that the client had a houseful of visitors – or that the client was on a cell phone in a car or restaurant. While the convenience and flexibility offered by Distance Counseling make it an attractive option, security and confidentiality should not be compromised.

When contacting clients online, counselors need to be mindful of style and tone as well as content of their communications. Counselors may be accustomed to using e-mail and chat or instant messaging for brief contact with friends, family, and colleagues, and may use informal language which makes use of abbreviations, lower case letters and symbols (a.k.a., emoticons). When communicating with clients, or potential clients, counselors are advised to be more conservative in their approach. There is potential for misunderstandings to arise if, for example, the client is not familiar with the "shorthand" used by the counselor. As the counselor gets to know the client better, it becomes easier to assess the appropriateness of using a more colloquial writing style. Further, a terse communication that may be perfectly acceptable when sent to a colleague could appear brusque or cold in tone to a client. Taking a moment to add a line or two to reflect caring and warmth may help to engage a client and convey the counselor's concern.

Clients may, at times, discuss or present with issues that seem beyond the scope of the counselor's expertise or the program's stated purpose. The counselor will need to handle these situations the same way they do in face-to-face practice; namely, by making appropriate referrals. This scenario can pose a challenge in Distance Counseling. Will the referral be for face-to-face services or distance services? If the counselor and client agree that face-to-face services are indicated, the counselor will need to identify resources in the client's geographical area. If appropriate services are not available in the client's locale, or if the client has a preference for distance services, the counselor will need to research options. In either case, the counselor will need to take steps to make the transition as smooth and comfortable for the client as possible. Due diligence and research of resources for such eventualities are important components of the planning process prior to the actual delivery of distance services to the client.

Time Factors

Many e-mail users find that time feels different in cyberspace. Fenichel (2002) discusses this phenomenon and the concept of *time-shifting* in his article "The Here and Now of Cyberspace." When a writer sends an e-mail, there may be an expectation that the recipient will respond immediately. If this doesn't happen, the sender may become anxious and wonder if the other person is angry, or ever received the communication. Ironically, the absence of cues that makes it easier for individuals to self-disclose may also lead to anxiety if responses are not received within an anticipated time frame. In reality, there may be any number of reasons for a delayed response: the recipient may be busy, or out of town or may be taking time to compose a thoughtful response. The recipient may not be aware of the sender's eagerness to receive a quick response. The two parties may simply have a different understanding of the time that "should" elapse between the receipt of a communication and its response.

Counselors may find that they need to maintain a delicate balance. On the one hand, they certainly intend to be respectful of the client's desire to be heard and helped; and they are mindful of any feelings of vulnerability that the client may be experiencing. On the other hand, counselors always maintain boundaries and ensure that the client does not become intrusive or overly demanding of their time. Again, clear and upfront information about frequency of communication and length of time between receipt of client e-mail and counselor response should be provided to the client before counseling begins. Once the counselor establishes these guidelines, it is imperative that both parties adhere to them. If the Distance Counseling modality involves online interaction, counselor and client must check e-mail on a daily basis and respond to messages in a timely fashion. If the counselor will be away from the office, this information needs to be conveyed to clients and potential clients, just as it would be in face-to-face practice.

The immediacy of electronic communication may influence people's notions of how the communication should be paced. Many of us are all too familiar with the phenomenon of the 24-hour office. If cell phones, pagers, e-mail, and instant messages make it possible for people to track one another down anytime, anywhere, then one might ask whether clients should be able to have 24-hour access to their counselors? Again, counselors have a responsibility to set and enforce reasonable limits on their availability and clearly communicate this information to clients. Counselors are also advised to provide emergency resources (e.g., 911, suicide hotline number) on their Web sites, answering machines, and voice mail so that clients have this information if they are not able to reach their counselors in time of crisis.

Cross-Cultural Factors

Just as in face-to-face practice, counselors need to be mindful of language and cultural differences. Because of the global nature of the Internet, it is possible that clients from other countries and cultures will seek out the services of a Distance Counselor. While this presents wonderful and enriching opportunities for both counselor and client, it also poses risks for miscommunication and misunderstanding. Ethical codes and standards for best practices dictate that counselors not deliver services beyond their scope of competency. Certainly, they may not represent themselves as experts in areas in which they lack education and experience. This admonition applies especially to cultural factors since technology significantly reduces geographical barriers.

This is not to say that a counselor should never attempt to work with a client of another cultural background. It is possible to hypothesize that any experienced counselor has dealt with a wide variety of clients in face-to-face practice. In face-to-face practice, however, it is likely that clients reside, at least temporarily, in the same geographical region as their counselors. A foreign student, for example, may seek the services of a college counselor while studying in the U.S. on a visa. In this case, the counselor will want to self-educate with respect to the client's country of origin and may need to clarify any matters that arise from linguistic or cultural issues. In addition, there will be visual cues to help resolve any misunderstandings that may arise during the counseling interaction.

In Distance Counseling, however, the possibilities for complications are increased when working with clients from other countries or cultures. To begin with, a client may intentionally seek out the services of a counselor residing in a different country. The counselor may, for example, have an area of expertise that is not represented in the client's own country. This may pose benefits for both client and counselor, but it also raises some challenging issues. Are both parties fluent in the same language? If not, in whose language will the counseling be conducted? Differing cultural values may also come into play here. How will payment be handled, and in what currency? Are there ethical or legal codes advising the counselor against international practice? Suler et al. (2001) offer the following caveat:

> It is very likely that the online clinician will receive requests for therapy by people from other countries and cultures. In these cases clinicians must determine whether communication will be significantly hindered by differences in language, and whether they are familiar enough with the person's culture in order to effectively conduct psychotherapy. Although cross-cultural issues are also important in in-person therapy, such issues may be unique and magnified in an online therapy when the client is living in a country that is geographically distant from the therapist. (p. 5)

I have had the great privilege of working with two clients in other countries through my association with ReadyMinds. In both cases, the clients were fluent in English and had lived and/or traveled in the U.S. The issues that they brought to the career counseling process were not culture-specific and the clients were able to explain, briefly, any local factors that differed from the job market or educational system in the U.S. The counseling was time-limited, structured, and overseen by a larger entity (i.e., ReadyMinds). I had access to supervision and support, both clinical and administrative. If I were working independently and a client from another country had sought out my services, the situation might have been quite different.

Any counselor considering work with clients in other countries is advised to seek supervision and/or consultation with an experienced Distance Counselor to determine whether or not to pursue this course of action. The counselor is also advised to contact any relevant credentialing and licensing agencies about regulations governing international counseling practice. As stated in Goss and Anthony (2003), there are certainly risks involved in this kind of counseling that do not exist in more locally-based forms of counseling.

Even if counselors are not working with clients in other countries, they may encounter clients from cultures or geographical locations different from their own. A client living in a rural area, for example, may seek the services of a city-based counselor. Although this situation may be less dramatic or extreme than the cross-cultural scenarios presented above, it may still present significant challenges to counselor and client. Again, counselors should assess their own level of preparedness to work with a client from a markedly different setting or culture. They will need to do research, test assumptions, and ask questions to avoid misconceptions and miscommunication. It will also be necessary to identify resources in the client's geographical area, and perhaps pertaining to the client's cultural background.

Emergency Situations

There is always the possibility, as there is in face-to-face counseling, that a client will threaten or attempt violence against self or another. These are scenarios that give rise to understandable anxiety in practitioners. When delivering Distance Counseling, it is even more incumbent upon a counselor or organization to develop a clear and detailed plan for dealing with emergency situations such as these. The plan should take into account relevant legal and ethical guidelines and include specific resources and supports that can be employed as needed. ReadyMinds has crafted the following carefully designed plan that receives focused attention during all of our various Distance Counseling training programs. With such a plan in place, counselors will have guidance and definite steps to follow so that they do not have the added pressure of developing a plan in time of crisis. Fortunately, after working with well over a hundred clients and case managing many more, I have never needed to implement the ReadyMinds suicide/homicide prevention plan. I am, however, relieved that this plan is in place in case I ever do encounter such a situation.

READYMINDS EMERGENCY COUNSELING PLAN

Strong Probability of *Harm to Self* (For ex., client says, I will take a bottle of pills tonight, If I don't hear from boyfriend tonight I will jump out the window)	Imminent Danger to *Self* (For ex., client says, I have a gun to my head right now, the window is open next to me and I feel like jumping)	Strong or Imminent Probability *of Harm to Another* (For ex., client says, I'm going to kill that math professor, he ruined my chances of getting into med school)
Ask the client to identify his/her location & area code, then call the operator (dial 0) or area code 1 555 1212 and ask for assistance in accessing the local emergency services for the client's location.	1. Attempt to keep client on phone. 2. Ask the client to identify his/her location and contact campus security using another phone. Ask the client to identify his/her location and area code, then call your operator (dial 0) or area code + 555 1212 and ask for assistance in accessing the local emergency services for the client's location 3. If Distance Counselor does not have immediate access to another phone line, alert the client that you will be hanging up, calling Campus Security or appropriate emergency resource and calling back. 4. Ask the client to wait by the phone to receive your return phone call.	1. Make every effort to immediately contact the threatened individual directly. 2. Inform local law enforcement authorities. If the counselor has no means of establishing contact with the threatened person (e.g. client threatens roommate whose name is not known to the counselor), the counselor will contact appropriate local law enforcement authorities immediately. 3. Inform client that you are reporting the threat.

Conclusion

After several years of practice, I can honestly say that the benefits of Distance Counseling outweigh its risks *for me*. I use this qualifier because I base the statement on my own experience; each counselor will need to assess individual comfort levels with distance modalities and their impact on scope of practice as well as professional preparation and training. Working within an established structure (i.e., the ReadyMinds program), with supports in place, has made the process more comfortable for me and given me tools for resolving any difficult situations that have arisen in the course of my counseling or case management work. Experience has certainly increased my confidence in my ability to manage the challenges that present themselves, and research into best practices has given me further guidance. With good preparation, support, and resourcefulness, the counselor may find that many challenges to Distance Counseling are far less daunting than might be imagined.

Counselor Tips for Taking Action

- *Prior to offering distance services, acquire appropriate competencies related to this evolving specialty through training and a thorough reading of related research and literature.*
- *Learn how to adapt face-to-face methods for effective application to Distance Counseling and understand the additional benefits that are unique to joining technology with counseling.*
- *Develop an effective mastery of the specific technologies you will employ when delivering distance services and ensure the support of either institutional or private technical resources.*
- *Screen clients for suitability with respect to the specific distance services you intend to use. This process includes an examination of the client's technical competencies.*
- *As part of a thorough informed consent process, educate your clients concerning the challenges and difficult situations that may occur during Distance Counseling. Help them to anticipate preventive measures as well as strategies to deal with special problems. Strategies for dealing with emergencies should be in the form of a written plan.*

- *As much as possible and based on thorough pre-counseling information, have in place referral information specific to each client's need prior to the commencement of actual counseling services.*
- *Become familiar with your professional association ethical guidelines for Distance Counseling that have been developed to inform your specific scope of practice.*
- *Perform appropriate due diligence with respect to legal issues and state licensure board sponsored regulatory policies that govern your specific practices when delivering distance services.*
- *Familiarize yourself with resources for support, case management and supervision, including your esteemed colleagues and professional associations, so that you may offer the highest level of distance counseling to your clients.*

Questions for Chapter Review

1) What measures can I take to prepare for the possibility of technical breakdowns during the distance counseling process?
2) What kinds of upfront information will I need to provide to my clients about the distance counseling process?
3) What strategies might I employ to compensate for the lack of visual cues in distance counseling?
4) How can I determine whether or not to work with clients of other cultures or countries?
5) How will I develop a plan to implement in case of emergency?

References

Chechele, P. J., & Stofle, G. (2003). Individual therapy online via e-mail and Internet relay chat. In S. Goss & K. Anthony (Eds.), *Technology in counseling and psychotherapy: A practitioner's guide* (pp. 39-58). Houndmills, UK: Palgrave Macmillan.

Fenichel, M. (2002). *The here and now of cyberspace*. Retrieved November 22, 2004, from http://www.fenichel.com/herenow.shtml

Goss, S., & Anthony, K. (2003). *Technology in counseling and psychotherapy: A practitioner's guide*. Houndsmills, UK: Palgrave Macmillan

Malone, J. F., & Miller, K. S. (2000). *The ReadyMinds career counselor training manual.* New York: ReadyMinds Internal Proprietary Training Document.

Rosenfield, M. (2003). Telephone counseling and psychotherapy in practice. In S. Goss & K. Anthony (Eds.), *Technology in counseling and psychotherapy: A practitioner's guide* (pp. 93-108). New York: Palgrave MacMillan.

Suler, J. (2001). *The online disinhibition effect.* Retrieved November 22, 2004, from http://www.rider.edu/~suler/psycyber/disinhibit.html

Suler, J., Barak, A., Chechele, P., Fenichel, M., Hsiung, R., Maguire, J., Meunier, V., Stofle, G., Tucker-Ladd, C., Vardell, M., & Walker-Schmucker, W. (2001). Assessing a person's suitability for online therapy. *CyberPsychology and Behavior, 4,* 675-80

CHAPTER ELEVEN

Ethical Guidelines, Legal and Regulatory Issues in Distance Counseling

James F. Malone

This chapter begins with a discussion of the concept of competency-based skills as they apply to matters of ethics, legality, and the regulation of Distance Counseling practices. Relevant resources provided by ReadyMinds and major counseling organizations and associations are described along with information on how counselors can access these resources. References to the literature are included as well as anecdotal discussion of inquiries to various state licensing boards. Specific ethical and legal issues are examined including: informed consent, client suitability, accessibility, counselor competencies, the Distance Credentialed Counselor (DCC) Training Program, technology-related challenges, Internet security, assessment via distance, and computerized counseling programs.

The following scenario provides a realistic situation in which a practicing counselor becomes more aware of the legal and ethical issues that surround distance delivery of counseling services:

> *John is a career counselor who works at a local community college. It is not at all uncommon for some of his students or alumni to seek assistance by telephone or via e-mail. They tend to prefer these communication methods; and, in fact, he has found that he is able to assist some individuals who would otherwise not visit his office to seek help. He has received anecdotal feedback that this type of counseling assistance is effective. It certainly seems to make sense. However, a recent article dealing with Distance Counseling (Heinlein, Welfel, Richmond, & Rak, 2003) got him thinking a bit more deeply about this kind of counseling theory. Several issues about technology and counseling are emerging,*

raising questions that he has not really thought a whole lot about. Here are some specific concerns that enter his mind:

- *How do I really know the identity of who I am communicating with? What if I mistakenly pass along grades or previous counseling information to an imposter or someone pulling a prank?*
- *Do these clients really understand the parameters of Distance Counseling and some of the limitations such as technical breakdowns or misunderstandings due to lack of visual cues?*
- *What happens in the case of an emergency or a need for timely follow-up with a distance client?*
- *Is my service available to all clients, e.g., to individuals with disabilities or limited access to technology?*
- *How secure is our e-mail communication, and what are the issues surrounding the use of cell phones?*
- *If alumni are in another state or geographical jurisdiction, are there implications for our conducting career counseling via distance methods?*

All of a sudden John is wondering about these and other issues that are addressed in the article. He also realizes he is not the only one who has engaged in distance methods of counseling without careful attention to these questions. The thrust of the article points out that there appears to be very poor counselor compliance with many of the ethical guidelines recommended by the National Board for Certified Counselors (NBCC) and other major counseling organizations regarding work with clients via distance methods. Where does he go to seek help so that he "does no harm" and may enjoy a level of professional comfort in providing his services via this promising delivery system?

Understanding the Dilemma

John's uncertainties are shared by many counselors in this age of advanced technology. Whether engaged in career-educational counseling or more clinical-psychological services, counselors are aware that their services, received by clients in institutional or private practice settings, must comply with ethical, legal, and regulatory guidelines. Anthony & Goss (2003) refer to the dilemma of offering services while the empirical research on such services is currently evolving. On the one hand, counselors feel the need to exercise caution. However, these same authors also make the case that withholding technology-assisted counseling services to populations who seek and could benefit from them might be considered an ethical breach in itself.

Ethics, Legalities and Regulatory Issues: Compliance

It makes sense at the outset of our discussion to offer some distinctions and clarifying comments regarding ethics, legalities, and regulatory issues since they deal with counselor practice and client protection from different points of view. They also tie in with credentialing processes such as certification and licensure as well as the entities that regulate practice as related to credentials. The "Resources" section of the American Counseling Association (ACA) Web site (http://www.counseling.org) offers excellent definitions and commentary regarding ethics, certification, and licensure, as well as detailed charts of state licensure requirements. The reader is strongly encouraged to review this important information.

Simply put, ethical codes present guidelines or guiding principles of right conduct that should govern the behavior of a given profession. In our case, counselors are advised regarding specific behaviors that protect the consumers or recipients of our professional services. Legal mandates are a different matter. These are laws established through governmental legislation. For example, state departments of education grant individuals licensure status carrying with it the right to practice their profession. Licensure issues and related policies governing practice are monitored by state licensure boards. The regulatory guidelines are the mandates that each state dictates to practitioners with respect to how they serve clients within their scope of practice or according to the title under which they practice within that state, and in some cases, beyond their state of residence. The majority of states regulate multiple forms of counseling by scope of practice (i.e., mental health, career, rehabilitation). However, others regulate counselor services by the title under which the counselor practices. States that regulate the practice of mental health counseling may or may not choose to regulate career or rehabilitation counseling.

While ethical guidelines are very important principles that should guide our professional behaviors, their violation may not necessarily incur a violation of law. However, since all ethical guidelines urge practitioners to practice within the law, any legal violation is a de facto ethical breach. As pointed out on the ACA Web site, licensure is a credentialing process that grants practitioners the legal right to offer specific services within their home state according to their training, education, supervised experience, and related fulfillment of requirements such as passing the National Counselor Exam (NCE). Certification, on the other hand, provides recognition, usually by a prestigious association on the state or national level, of the practitioner's having met certain requirements related to education and experience. As is the case with the NBCC, the passing of a major comprehensive exam, the NCE, is also required. Certification status is primarily an endorsement that the individual is in good standing to practice within the profession; but it does not carry with it the legal right to offer services. Certain complicated issues, such as portability of licensure and the ambiguities inherent in offering distance services from state to state, will be discussed later in this chapter.

One might wonder how Internet sites that offer online services comply with ethical standards. The article mentioned at the beginning of this chapter found that while professional counselors with licenses and degrees had a significantly higher rate of compliance than individuals with no such credentials, there was still a very low overall level of compliance with the NBCC Standards; not a single site enjoyed full compliance (Heinlein, Welfel, Richmond, & Rak, 2003). This sampling of the Web sites took place in 1999 and 2000. In addition, it examined only sites offering Web-based services.

A more recent study (Shaw & Shaw, 2006) took another critical look at how compliant current Distance Counseling practices fared with existing ethical guidelines. While some improvements are noted, the overall results and conclusions of the study are equally sobering and indicate many areas in need of improvement.

During the several years ReadyMinds spent building its own Web site and related Distance Counseling services, the counseling and technical architects paid consistent attention to available research as well as to ethical, legal, and regulatory guidelines. All ReadyMinds Career Counseling and Planning Training Handbooks (Malone & Miller, 2000) focus heavily on counseling competencies and relating these skills to training experiences that adhere to recommended ethical guidelines. In designing the Distance Credentialed Counselor (DCC) Training Handbook (Malone, Miller, &

Ravis, 2003), ReadyMinds framed the training modules around 22 specific counseling competencies that apply to offering Distance Counseling. Among the 22 DCC competencies, one finds skills such as being able to adapt effective face-to-face counseling skills for distance delivery, knowing how to screen clients for suitability, and being able to demonstrate appropriate knowledge about the effective use of various forms of technology. DCC competencies address issues that relate to ensuring excellence of care to clients. In that sense, they all address ethical issues implicitly; and many legal implications are embedded throughout as well. However, the following two competencies address ethical, legal, and regulatory issues explicitly:

Counselors know how to apply ethical guidelines and standards relevant to Distance Counseling in their respective fields of practice.

Counselors know where to find resources on legal guidelines and standards relevant to their specific Distance Counseling specialties in their states and jurisdictions.

Professional Associations

Several points can be made here with respect to the counselor's responsibilities to clients and to themselves as members of the profession. First, counselors need to know what these ethical guidelines are and where to find them. Most of the professional organizations have published ethical codes that address technology-assisted counseling services under the rubrics of WebCounseling, Online Counseling, Cybercounseling, or Distance Counseling.

Consulting counselor association Websites will yield informative resources. For example, in its revised Code of Ethics the American Counseling Association (ACA) addresses "Technology Applications" under Standard A.12. The National Board for Certified Counselors (NBCC) presents "The Practice of Internet Counseling". In accordance with their counseling specialties and scopes of practice, counselors should research these resources in addition to those offered by the National Career Development Association (NCDA), the International Society for Mental Health Online (ISMHO), and the American Psychological Association (APA).

Additional organizations and Web links may be found in the Appendix to a very recent article by Harris-Bowlsbey and Sampson (2005). The authors offer a comprehensive treatment of technology-assisted counseling services on the international level, and they address specific issues such as client readiness and important resources including the use of Web sites.

In general, these guidelines address issues such as client suitability and identity management, informed consent regarding the nature and structure of offered services, strategies to cover misunderstandings or emergencies, specific technology issues such as maintaining confidentiality and related security measures, encryption, and finally, legal and jurisdictional information including clients' rights of redress. Counselors need to be familiar with these guidelines within the context of their work settings and scopes of practice. When questions arise regarding the application of a specific ethical issue, it is always advisable to check with supervisors, esteemed peers, and the association's ethics advisors for clarification.

Regarding the legal issues, a survey of States Attorney Generals by Koocher and Morray (2000) and a survey inquiry to state licensure boards by Bloom and Sampson (2000) represent efforts towards seeking some type of overview information regarding each individual state's regulatory management of Distance Counseling services offered by specific technologies on both interstate and intrastate levels. It is not the role or intent of this chapter to offer legal opinions or to provide definitive resolutions regarding ambiguous ethical and legal dilemmas. We intend rather to frame the issues and extend information to assist readers in making inquiries to the formal resources that range from the designated contacts within counseling associations and state licensing boards, to the literature, and finally, to their supervisors and esteemed colleagues for professional consultation.

It is worth mentioning that other industries face similar questions and restrictions on offering services between states. The practice of telemedicine, now considered by many to be a useful and effective way of diagnosing, treating, and monitoring certain patient conditions, is receiving a great deal of attention from state medical boards and legislatures.

Specific Issues

Here is a sampling of some specific issues that one typically finds mentioned among ethical guidelines.

Informed Consent

Just as in face-to-face counseling services, clients need to be fully informed about the nature of the Distance Counseling services they will receive. A clear explanation including Terms and Conditions presented in a clear and accessible communication format needs to be provided. A well-designed Web site allows the client to understand in practical ways what the service entails and how it is to be delivered. Concrete discussions of counseling delivered by telephone, e-mail, chat, or videoconferencing must be fully explained. Related issues such as privacy, confidentiality, legal and ethical questions, grievances, termination, fee structure, and all other appropriate questions should be addressed.

ReadyMinds has created examples of "informed consent" communications on its Web site so that clients can understand the specific services offered within its various career counseling and career planning programs. Clients are required to read each section before registering for a service level. They are also advised fully of their rights, duties, and expected ethical behaviors. Please see the example of ReadyMinds Informed Consent provided in Chapter Two of this publication.

Client Suitability

It is essential that there is a good match between client and counselor. Current discussions about client suitability suggest various opinions regarding which clients are most suited for Distance Counseling services. There is universal agreement that thorough and careful client screening is essential in order to be sure the counselor's experience and expertise within his/her scope of practice matches the client's counseling needs. At one end of the spectrum, we may read that highly anxious or severely depressed individuals are not good candidates because they need more intensive and personalized care. On the other hand, one reads opinions (Fenichel, Suler, Barak, Zelvin, Jones, Munro, Meunier, & Walker-Schmucker, 2002) that severely disturbed clients may actually profit from some of the advantages that Distance Counseling has to offer such as the immediate access to a counselor during times of high need. ReadyMinds counseling practitioners report that, absent any significant emotional problems, candidates for career counseling do realize benefits from a Distance Counseling experience. These assertions receive robust support via the client satisfaction surveys that clients complete upon termination of their counseling contacts. Professional common sense dictates that counselor and client need to discuss openly and honestly what the client's needs are and determine whether a Distance Counseling delivery model of services will be helpful, keeping in mind the mandate "do no harm."

Distance Counselors will refer clients to other or additional counseling resources if they determine such a need either before or while delivering their own services. A site such as Metanoia (http://www.metanoia.org/suicide) is an example of an appropriate resource in cases of extreme need. It is also necessary as part of the registration and due diligence process preceding the actual delivery of counseling that the counselor obtains emergency contact information for each client.

Client Access and Financial Capability

Access to technology includes economic concerns relating to the digital divide. If clients are unable to afford services, ethical mandates dictate that the counselor assist in locating appropriate referrals for either low cost or free public access to services. However, Peterson (2003) makes the point that it is frequently and precisely Distance Counseling services that are financially friendly to persons with high economic need.

Counselor's Professional Credentials, Competence,
and Training; Client Technology Skills

Clearly, counselors are expected to offer services within the limits of their scope of practice. They are governed by the ethical standards of their professional associations and the legal requirements of licensure laws within their states. Specific training, such as that required for administering certain counseling assessments or special skills needed for Distance Counseling should be sought and completed before delivering such services. A realistic description of essential technology as well as communication skills should be provided to potential clients in the interests of suitability so they may choose distance delivery options from an informed point of view. How well do they express themselves in writing? Can they handle live chat communication? Career counselors need to be aware that the adaptation of effective face-to-face techniques to distance delivery calls for additional preparation such as that offered by the Distance Credentialed Counselor

(DCC) Training Program. For example, telephone counseling tends to be more structured than face-to-face counseling and requires more active and discerning listening skills. Adaptation of spoken verbal counseling behaviors to a written format requires training and practice. These new skills may be learned or enhanced by specific training exercises.

Confidentiality of Communications: Servers, Phones, Faxes, Computers, E-mail, Electronic Records

Maheu, Pulier, Wilhelm, McMenamin, & Brown-Connolly (2005), Peterson (2003), Tyler and Sabella (2004), and Zack (2004) offer comprehensive treatments of counseling technology issues. Topics include all of the above delivery media including a discussion of the need for validated software for computer-assisted assessment products. One should not assume that assessment instruments that are validated for paper and pencil use may simply be rendered into software packages or placed on the Internet. There is a need for either equivalency studies or actual separate validation for computer/Internet delivered versions. Other professionals raise the issues of validation, licensing, and stricter regulation of self-help software in computer-assisted counseling programs for both career and mental health clients (Cavanagh, Zack, Shapiro, & Wright, 2003; Ford, 1993; Sampson, Kolodinsky, & Greeno, 1997). Technical competencies and housekeeping issues surround the use of various technologies for both counselor and clients. Cell phones and certain cordless phones are not considered secure, but this issue becomes increasingly more complex since many individuals use cell phones exclusively. Fax machines must be monitored carefully so that documents are received only by their intended recipients. Firewall and encryption technology add layers of protection, but practitioners must still protect access to records by maintaining vigilance in how they store information and maintain their office practices.

Cultural Sensitivity

While the importance of cultural sensitivity remains very much the same in both face-to-face and in Distance Counseling practices, the global reach of the latter option certainly invites greater potential for challenge. Therefore, it makes sense for counselors to restrict distance practice to clients from cultural backgrounds that are familiar, or certainly to do due diligence and appropriate preparation when offering services to individuals from cultures that are truly different from one's own. Intake questionnaires and surveys may contain an invitation to share cultural and ethnic background information, but such inquiries ought to be accompanied by a statement that indicates the intent of seeking this information is to enhance the counselor's awareness of the client's background in order to provide more informed service.

Rights of Redress

Clients have a legal right to redress if they feel appropriate standards of practice have not been maintained and have led to personal harm. Before the actual counseling begins, they should be given access to the ethical practices resources and contact information of the associations that govern the practitioner's professional behavior. These issues may become more complex, however, when different standards or expectations may exist due to geographical differences such as a counselor and client in different states or a counselor practicing in the United States and a client who received services in an international location. The state board where the client resides will not likely possess any jurisdictional power over the state where the counselor is practicing. There also remains some ambiguity with respect to where the actual counseling does take place; that is, in the counselor's location or in the client's location, or in both locations. Some state licensing boards are now making explicit statements that they consider the counseling as occurring in the state where the client resides, thereby indicating a requirement that the non-resident counselor possess appropriate dual licensure.

Additional Legal Considerations

Because Distance Counseling is relatively new, the legal profession has addressed interstate distance practice boundaries in a limited way. Attorney Jeffrey Love (2000) has offered an insightful treatment of these issues and the risks involved. He makes the point that well-trained and ethically conscious cybercounselors, not charlatans or impostors, may be hesitant to engage in interstate work out of a fear of prosecution based on severely restrictive local laws. In effect, such universally prohibitive policies might simply trump the ability of this evolving specialty to bring potential benefits to clients at a time when technology, appropriately managed, seems able to expand solutions and options for individuals who wish to exercise their full freedom of choice to seek counseling help regardless of their geographical location.

It must also be stated that related issues such as licensure and restrictions of services from one state to another are dependent to some degree on the nature of the counseling offered. Certainly there are more restrictions on professionals offering psychotherapy than on those offering career counseling. Professional organizations and state licensing boards have begun to explore reciprocity of licensure and portability plans to assist counselors who move from one jurisdiction to another. Recent reports from the NBCC (2005) and the ACA (Kennedy, 2006) cite progress in these efforts. The American Association of State Counseling Boards (AASCB) and the American Counseling Association (ACA) have been examining strategies to alleviate the long held concerns that counselors have expressed with respect to the maze of differing state requirements and licensure reciprocity. These concerns are driven not only by the possibility of elective relocation and residence change on the part of professional counselors. Experienced counselors, licensed in their former states, may face additional hardships such as expense and additional supervision requirements when relocating. We have also seen situations such as national disasters where rapid counselor response teams face a possible legal conflict when offering emergency services to their fellow Americans.

Since 2005, the National Credentials Registry (NCR) has offered a mechanism for counselors to warehouse documentation of their professional experience along with educational and work history, including supervision. As needed, counselors may then petition the NCR to provide official documentation to whichever state licensure board may be involved as the counselor's target destination. Full operational details of the Registry and additional information regarding individual state licensure boards and the portability of licensure plan may be found on the AASCB Web site (www.aascb.org).

As mentioned earlier, Koocher and Morray (2000) and Bloom and Sampson (2000) did seminal surveys regarding these issues. At the current time, there is no known list of each state's policies. Therefore, counselors are advised to check into the licensing requirements of their own states and those of potential clients. Discussion among esteemed colleagues and professional peers has also raised the issues of the counselor's work setting as well as the scope of practice, and how these factors may influence the application of restrictions related to licensure and jurisdiction. Depending on location, institutional affiliation, and counseling service, career counselors working with universities and governmental agencies may encounter different kinds of limitations on their distance work than solo private practitioners since they are working within a tightly organized program design which enjoys case management and supervisor oversight on a regular basis.

Closing Remarks

The practical and psychological advantages of technology-assisted forms of Distance Counseling continue to receive considerable anecdotal support with some promising empirical studies adding greater credibility (Anthony & Goss, 2003). At the same time, this modality is not appropriate for all clients, as pointed out by Kraus (2004), when discussing the limitations of online counseling work in the context of ethical and legal considerations.

The ongoing challenge here is for counselors to navigate the ambiguities of a promising and evolving specialty that offers convenient as well as helpful service. Professional counselors need to inform themselves and their clients with respect to ethical and legal obligations. Currently, the best resources for doing so appear to lie with their professional organizations and associations, state licensing and regulatory boards, and continued dialogue with esteemed colleagues and peers. For example, clinical counselors may seek online discussion with peers through the International Society of Mental Health Online (ISMHO). Their mission, as described on their Web site (http://www.ismho.org), is "to promote the understanding, use and development of online communication, information, and technology for the international mental health community." Counselors may also seek wisdom from a considerable body of literature on Distance Counseling that grows weekly. An excellent source is the Distance Counseling Bibliography developed by Shy and Sampson (2006) at the Center for the Study of Technology in Counseling and Career Development at Florida State. Counselors may also seek out ongoing workshops and more formalized training through the Distance Credentialed Counselor Training Program available through ReadyMinds.

When faced with questions about legal and ethical issues in Distance Counseling, we recommend that counselors consult the following resources:

Professional Counselor Organizations (Ethics Officers)
Ethical Guides

State Licensure Organizations
Professional Literature
Attorneys and related Legal Resource
Esteemed Colleagues

Counselor Tips for Taking Action

- *Understand and appreciate the differences between ethical guidelines and legal/regulatory mandates.*
- *Become familiar with, and adhere to, the ethical guidelines of the professional organizations in which you hold professional membership.*
- *Observe the legal and regulatory mandates of the jurisdictions that govern your scope and location of practice.*
- *Seek clarification and support from supervisors, association personnel, attorneys, and esteemed colleagues when you face ambiguities that may occur in your practice of Distance Counseling.*
- *Take appropriate precautions and plan your distance services carefully in order to ensure best care to clients with respect to issues such as: screening for client suitability; identity management; contingency and emergency communication plans, including available referral resources; potential misunderstandings and technology failures; potential threats to privacy and confidentiality; informed consent regarding all counseling related services including fee structures/insurance coverage and, if necessary, access to free public counseling services; electronic security measures and practices; client communication and technology competence; special needs with respect to abilities; sensitivity to language and cultural needs; rights of redress and access to information regarding certification and licensing boards; maintenance of records and release of information practices; validity and reliability of assessment and Web site information.*

Questions and Scenarios for Chapter Review

Consider these questions as an "Activity Quiz"

1. A client contacts you with the results of career interest and personal style "tests" he found on the Internet. He is a client that you counsel privately

in a face-to-face setting, and he wants help in interpreting the assessment results. What obligations should you meet before engaging this individual in any type of assessment interpretation?

2. You are working in a university career services office and alumni are welcome to contact you spontaneously either by telephone or e-mail in order to receive assistance with career counseling or career planning issues. An individual contacts you and mentions that some mental health issues (depression and anxiety) are interfering with her career planning efforts but she would still like to access your distance services. How would you proceed with this person?

3. You are a private practitioner doing career counseling and a client wants to engage you in continued work even though she is moving out of your state. You are aware that you do not need to be licensed in your own state to conduct career counseling. What additional considerations should you research before agreeing to offer continued services?

4. You offer mental health/clinical counseling over the Internet and have your own Web site. A client begins the registration process and then contacts you with the news that he can't afford your stated fees although he became really motivated about engaging your services. How should you respond to this client?

5. You are offering e-mail-supported career counseling to students at your university. You receive an e-mail inquiry from a student who identifies himself as someone with whom you have had previous contact. This individual is asking that some assessment results and accompanying academic information be forwarded to them. How can you be sure that you are not dealing with an impostor or a prankster?

6. You and a group of counseling colleagues are thinking about offering career and mental health counseling services through a distance model. Rather than starting up entirely on your own, you are entertaining the possibility of accessing already existing distance delivery platforms. Your research has led you to several Web sites and conversations with peers suggest that the following are promising possibilities; http://www.letstalkcounseling.com and http://www.asktheinternettherapist.com. What kinds of criteria do you apply to evaluating these sites when deciding if you might want to offer services through them?

References

Anthony, K., & Goss, S. (2003). Conclusion. In S. Goss & K. Anthony (Eds.), *Technology in counseling and psychotherapy: A practitioner's guide* (pp 195-207). Houndmills, UK: Palgrave Macmillan.

Bloom, J. W., & Sampson, J. P., Jr. (2000). *Telephone counseling and cybercounseling survey.* Tampa, FL: Report issued to the 2001 AASCB Conference.

Cavanaugh, K., Zack, J. S., Shapiro, D. A., & Wright, J.A. (2003). Computer programs for psychotherapy. In S. Goss & K. Anthony (Eds.), *Technology in counseling and psychotherapy: A practitioner's guide* (pp. 143-164). Houndmills, UK: Palgrave Macmillan.

Fenichel, M., Suler, J., Barak, A., Zelvin, E., Jones, G., Munro, K., Meunier, V., & Walker-Schmucker, W. (2002). Myths and realities of online clinical work. Retrieved September 23, 2005, from http://www.rider.edu/~suler/psycyber/myths.html

Ford, B. D. (1993). In Peterson, D. B. (2003). Ethics and technology. In R. R. Cottone., & V.M. Tarvydas (Eds). *Ethical and professional issues in counseling* (2nd ed.) (pp. 169-200). Upper Saddle River, NJ: Merrill/Prentice-Hall.

Harris-Bowlsbey, J., & Sampson, J.P., Jr. (2005). Use of technology in delivering career services worldwide. *The Career Development Quarterly, 54,* 48-56.

Heinlein, K. T., Welfel, E. R., Richmond, E. N., & Rak, C. F. (2003). The scope of WebCounseling: A survey of services and compliance with NBCC standards for the ethical practice of WebCounseling. *Journal of Counseling and Development, 81,* 61- 69.

Kennedy, A. (2006). Licensure portability update announced at convention. *Counseling Today,* 8.

Koocher, G., & Morray, E. (2000). Regulation of telepsychology: A survey of state attorneys general. *Professional Psychology: Research and Practice, 31,* 503-508.

Kraus, R. (2004). Ethical and legal considerations for providers of mental health services online. In R. Kraus, J. Zack, & G. Stricker (Eds.), *Online counseling: A handbook for mental health professionals* (pp. 123-144). San Diego, CA: Elsevier Academic Press.

Love, J. (2000). Cybercounselors v. cyberpolice. In J. W. Bloom, & G. R. Walz (Eds.), *Cybercounseling and cyberlearning: Strategies and resources for the new millennium* (pp. 339-360). Alexandria, VA: American Counseling Association.

Maheu, M. M., Pulier, M. L, Wilhelm, F. H, McMenamin, J. P. & Brown-Connolly, N. E. (2005). *The mental health professional and the new technologies: A handbook for practice today.* Mahwah, NJ: Lawrence Erlbaum Associates.

Malone, J. F., & Miller, K. S. (2000). *ReadyMinds distance career counselor training handbook.* New York: Ready & Motivated Minds, LLC.

Malone, J. F., Miller, K. S. & Ravis H. (2003). *ReadyMinds distance credentialed counselor training handbook.* Lyndhurst, NJ: Ready & Motivated Minds, LLC.

National Board for Certified Counselors. (2005). AASCB presents the national credentials registry. *The National Certified Counselor, Fall Issue,* 8.

Peterson, D. B. (2003). Ethics and technology. In R. R. Cottone., & V. M. Tarvydas (Eds), *Ethical and professional issues in counseling* (2nd ed.) (pp. 169-200). Upper Saddle River, NJ: Merrill/Prentice-Hall.

Sampson, J. P., Jr., Kolodinsky, R. W., & Greeno, B. P. (1997). Counseling on the information highway: Future possibilities and potential problems. *Journal of Counseling and Development, 75,* 203-212.

Shaw, H. E., & Shaw, S. F., (2006). Critical ethical issues in online counseling: Assessing current practices with an ethical intent checklist. *Journal of Counseling & Development, 84,* 41-53.

Shy, J. D., & Sampson, J. P. (2006). *Distance counseling bibliography.* Retrieved September 25, 2005) from http://www.career.fsu.edu/documents/bibliographies/Distance%20Counseling_7_21.htm

Tyler, J. M., & Sabella, R. (2004). *Using technology to improve counseling practice: A primer for the 21st century.* Alexandria, VA: American Counseling Association.

Zack, J. S., (2003). Technology of online counseling. In R. Kraus, J. Zack, & G. Stricker (Eds.), *Online counseling: A handbook for mental health professionals.* San Diego, CA: Elsevier Academic Press.

CHAPTER TWELVE

Ensuring the Quality of Distance Counseling

Edwin Schwartz

This chapter describes the ReadyMinds process for evaluating, improving, and maintaining the quality of services delivered via Distance Counseling. Topics addressed include: Assessing counselor performance and appropriately sharing feedback; gathering valuable input from clients; and sharing evaluation data with an appropriate third party or sponsoring organization. The importance of ensuring quality is highlighted as it relates to providing best services for the client as well as establishing proper business practices.

Providing high quality service is a task that is of utmost importance to the client, the counselor, and to the counseling organization. Following proper counseling and business related procedures ensures that clients receive beneficial services and that counselors delivering the service experience continued growth and development within the scope of Distance Counseling. Additionally, proper planning and accurate assessment of services, along with following the proper ethical and legal guidelines for Distance Counseling, ensure that acceptable results will occur. These procedures will clearly and positively impact the "business of counseling."

Counselor Assessment

Whether one is a single practitioner or a part of a larger group or institution, receiving proper feedback from an appropriate supervisory individual, one in a position to evaluate your work, is of utmost importance. Additionally, "hearing" what your clients have to say about the service you provided can only serve to improve the delivery and content of your counseling services. Many questions surface surrounding best methodology and ethical concerns regarding the gathering of this information.

Distance Counseling

At ReadyMinds, specially trained counselors work beneath a hierarchy of support and management. From a business perspective, this structure is in place to ensure that each client receives the best possible delivery of service. The shared result of this process enables our counselors to develop and improve their skills as professionals who provide distance services.

Each ReadyMinds Counselor is assigned a Case Manager who, depending upon the experience level of the Distance Counselor involved, works very closely with the counselor. In every case, when counselors first begin delivering counseling via distance methodologies, it is important that they have an additional pair of eyes and ears to help them reflect upon their work. Each counselor involved with ReadyMinds is closely monitored for a minimum of the first two Distance Counseling cases assigned. As is the case with many supervisory relationships, when mutual comfort levels increase, the closeness and frequency of the supervision is adjusted accordingly. During the supervision of the first two cases, or more infrequently during subsequent cases, it may become apparent to a Case Manager that a counselor demonstrates serious deficiencies in core competencies. If this situation occurs, the Case Manager then consults with the Director of Counseling and discusses possible supportive interventions. After this consultation, the Case Manager speaks with the counselor involved and offers possible solutions such as additional training to remedy the situation. If the counselor and Case Manager do not reach an appropriate level of agreement, or if the counselor's performance does not improve over time, the advisability of mutually discontinuing the relationship between the counselor involved and ReadyMinds must then be considered.

It is an integral part of the ReadyMinds philosophy that Case Managers provide candid and constructive feedback to ReadyMinds Counselors. Once the case management relationship has been established, this feedback isprovided on a regular basis as requested by either the counselor or the Case Manager. In addition, periodic evaluation conferences are scheduled. In the case of ReadyMinds, Case Mangers meet with their counselors (using distance techniques, of course) every six months to provide appropriate feedback and support. Case Mangers themselves participate in a specific training at which time counselor performance criteria and competencies profiles are discussed and then utilized in a future supervision/management capacity.

During the performance evaluation sessions with a counselor, the supervisor/manager strives to achieve the following objectives:

1. To ensure that all appropriate counseling related forms have been properly completed.
2. To share client feedback.
3. To discuss the effectiveness of any written communications that may have occurred.
4. To discuss counselor's management of caseload.
5. To determine that the counselor is aware of environmental factors (current career literature and occupational, educational and employment trends).
6. To discuss the maintaining of timely and efficient communications with colleagues.

The following is a good example of feedback provided from a Case Manager to a Distance Counselor. It has been rendered anonymous for the purposes of this chapter.

Dear Mary,

Thank you for the preparation and time that went into making our recent Evaluation Conference so successful. It was a personal and professional pleasure to discuss your career counseling and planning work with our clients, as well as to review the business relationship you share with our organization.

Mary, based on our conversation, we agreed that you are doing excellent work with our clients. Your satisfaction surveys have been very strong, with scores in all categories averaging between 7 and 10 (with 10 being the highest possible score). As we discussed, the comments that clients made on the surveys indicate that they have found you to be empathic and focused on their needs. They report that you have given them useful resources and aided them in coming up with viable strategies for making their job searches more effective.

Another quality which has impressed me is the care that you take in preparing your Career Guidance Summaries. Your summaries are thorough, perceptive, and beautifully written, and include a number of appropriate resources. I am sure that your clients appreciate your thoughtful approach to the preparation of these important documents. This characteristic has helped to make you a highly respected member of our counseling staff. I know that we can rely on you to use good judgment in managing your caseload and schedule.

In addition, we discussed some areas for further development. We came up with ideas for helping you to establish realistic timetables for client goals (e.g., enlisting the client's aid in setting dates). We also talked about strategies for keeping your knowledge of local area resources and labor market information current. I am confident that you will handle these tasks with the professionalism that you bring to all other aspects of your work.

Mary, I also appreciate the data you shared with me regarding your own experience in offering career counseling and planning via a distance model. This information will help us in our continuous research efforts to improve the delivery model.

In closing, I would like to reiterate that I am always available to you for ongoing Case Management needs. Robert and John are also ready at any time to supplement my support so that we may continue to offer the highest possible quality of career counseling and guidance to our organization's clients.

The anticipated date of our next evaluation is six months from now. I will be in touch with you well before that date so that we may prepare for the conversation.

Again, thank you for all your hard work and professionalism. It is truly a pleasure to work with you.

Mary, please reply back to me to confirm that you have received this letter. Thank you.

Sincerely,
Emily
Case Manager

This hierarchical model of case management works very well when one is a counselor practicing as a member of a group. In most, if not all cases, a trained colleague can also serve responsibly in the role of a "peer consultant." What happens, however, when one is a single practitioner? In this case, finding the proper individual to provide appropriate feedback can certainly be more challenging. If one has been trained in Distance Counseling by attending a Distance Credentialed Counseling Training, jointly developed and sponsored by the National Board for Certified Counselors (NBCC) and ReadyMinds, opportunity to interact with many other counselors practicing Distance Counseling is provided. Contact information is shared (when agreed upon) and often a supporting relationship can be developed among co-attendees. Additionally, organizations such as the International Society for Mental Health Online (ISHMO) and The Association for Counselor Education and Supervision (ACES) can at times provide support and supervision.

In the case of ISHMO, DeeAnna Merz, President of ISHMO for 2005, has indicated that this opportunity for consultation has proven to be a beneficial and valuable aspect of membership. The Association for Counselor Education and Supervision (ACES) is composed of personnel engaged in the professional preparation of counselors and individuals responsible for the ongoing supervision of counselors. ACES is a founding division of the American Counseling Association (ACA) and, as such, adheres to ACA's current ethical standards and to general codes of competence adopted throughout the mental health community. In response to numerous inquiries, and as the entire distance counseling area continues to grow and expand, ReadyMinds is considering the use of DCC Trainers and experienced Distance Counselors to provide supervision for a broader based counselor population, as needed.

Assessing Client Satisfaction

In whatever setting we may find ourselves, we very often are in a position of asking the famous question former New York City Mayor Edward Koch so often posed, "How am I doing?" As counselors, it is certainly invaluable to ascertain the answer to this question by receiving candid feedback from your client population.

During face-to-face counseling, feedback can be received in the moment or at the conclusion of a session or relationship. How can this same important information be gathered via distance? We must utilize the same "distance" skills that are used throughout the working relationship with a distance client. Effective communication, carefully constructed written words, and organized, efficient follow-up are essential.

At ReadyMinds, the conclusion of any service level program triggers a notification to the client indicating the great value placed on the feedback that clients can provide. In this follow-up communication, instructions are provided and the request is made for the client to spend between 5-10 minutes completing an easily accessible satisfaction survey. It is important to word this request carefully to encourage the client's candid response while providing a clear explanation of confidentiality practices. Clients should be informed that, under certain circumstances, their comments may be viewed with the counselor or other supervisory or management members of the organization.

ReadyMinds has found that when both quantitative and qualitative responses can be obtained, the feedback gathered is very rich and informative. It is important to gain insight into not only the perceived outcome of the counseling relationship, but also the client's thoughts surrounding the process for achieving such results. In gathering quantitative responses, certain numerical themes emerge regarding the client's perception of counselor skills as well as the value of the counseling experience. When evaluating these responses, care must be given not to overreact to any one response or any one survey. However, if a pattern emerges, it must be addressed.

The qualitative feedback received is very often of equal value and often offers increased benefit. Though one should take care not to jump to conclusions based on any one comment, it is appropriate to evaluate and address numerous comments that do form an overall picture. Two questions that are part of the ReadyMinds Client Satisfaction Survey have proven to be particularly valuable in the continuous development of the program as well as in assisting in counselor growth. The question is asked of each client, "Please describe three things that you felt were most effective and helpful about the ReadyMinds Program." This question has often resulted in specific and candid comments that have assisted ReadyMinds in the continuous improvement of its programs. The second question that allows for open-ended feedback is provided with the inquiry, "Please share with us any suggestions that you feel would improve the quality of the ReadyMinds Program." The responses to this question have provided the single most concrete area for valued feedback. Rewording this particular question to fit your working environment will enable you to receive important client feedback.

Historically, satisfaction surveys have a relatively small return rate. Think of your own lives and the times that you are asked to complete such surveys. How often do you actually take the time to return such requests? At ReadyMinds, depending upon the population being serviced, 15-20% of participants typically respond. Although a larger return rate would certainly be welcome and of value, we do consider the present rate of return to be above average and appreciate the valuable information that is gathered from the feedback we receive. Case Managers address specific counselor behaviors that emerge as "in need of attention" based on satisfaction surveys. Business-related concerns are addressed by the Vice President of Operations and the Director of Counseling. Dynamics and related expenses associated with this satisfaction area do play a major role in improving client satisfaction.

Sharing Feedback with a Third Party

In many cases, a client who is participating in career counseling has an association in some capacity with a third party. This relationship can be in the form of a student/institution relationship, employee/employer situation, or perhaps a third party sponsor or payee for the service. An ethical question often arises in these situations pertaining to what, if anything, can specifically be shared, and with whom. You must also consider the reasons for this request.

It is the belief of ReadyMinds and is, in fact, company policy, that no information can be shared without the consent of the individual being counseled. This guideline applies not only to the actual content of the counseling that occurs, but also applies to more generic information such as the fact that an individual is even involved in a counseling relationship. There are, however, times when information can and should be shared. In those cases, as mentioned, the individual involved must complete a release of counseling information consent form.

Depending upon the type of request for information that is made, different forms should be used. The proper approach is to be as specific as possible with the information requested. For example, if a company is paying for an individual to receive services, it is not unreasonable (assuming the client has granted permission) for that company to know that the person involved has, in fact, participated in the counseling service. In this case, a form (completed in advance of the counseling actually occurring) should be completed by the individual obtaining the service, indicating that he or she is giving permission to share concrete factual information with a particular company. Information such as the number and dates of the counseling sessions and the outcome as it may relate solely to employment is appropriate information to share. If a case arises in which a third party requests more specific information, then the exact information that will be shared should be clearly outlined and agreed to by the client. Similarly, when an academic institution is involved and budgetary concerns are a factor, when agreed upon, basic service information and statistics would be appropriately shared. When a sponsoring individual is asked to be involved in the receipt of information, it is critically important that in advance of services, the client agrees upon the exact information that will potentially be shared.

Counselor Tips for Taking Action

- *Commit yourself to an appropriate methodology that seeks candid evaluation of your distance services to clients.*
- *Design your own client satisfaction surveys, if sole practitioners, or work with your case management supervisors in institutional settings in order to arrive at appropriate strategies to seek feedback from clients.*
- *Depending on your work setting, you should engage in regular and appropriate case management communications with experienced professionals who can help you to evaluate the effectiveness of your services in this evolving specialty.*
- *Seek out ongoing support and communication with your esteemed colleagues, peers who are practicing Distance Counseling, as well as from your professional associations.*
- *Design instruments such as client satisfaction surveys clearly and present clients with transparent policies with respect to privacy, confidentiality, and opportunities for informed consent in cases where counseling information might be shared with third parties.*

Questions for Chapter Review

1. What benefits can be gained by properly managing the counseling process and the counselors involved?
2. In evaluating a Distance Counselor, what are some of the objectives of the evaluation process?
3. What sources are available to a private practitioner seeking supervision?
4. In assessing client satisfaction, how can one adhere to confidentiality guidelines as they relate to the sharing of the feedback received?
5. What steps can be taken ethically to share client information/feedback with a third party?
6. What are the risks that a counselor faces with little or no case management/supervision when servicing clients via distance?

APPENDIX A

The Use of Telephone Helplines in Career Information and Guidance

A.G. Watts & Gareth Dent

The UK Learndirect helpline, launched in February 1998, is the largest telephone helpline service in the guidance field. By the end of 2000 it had responded to 2.4 million calls; by late 2006 the figure had risen to over 8 million. This chapter, based on an article originally published in the *British Journal of Guidance and Counselling* in 2002, places the development of the helpline in the context of the transformations in service delivery in other sectors, including the growth of call centers and helplines. The current operation of the service is outlined, including its extent, availability, staffing, and users. Finally, a number of issues illuminated by the experiences of Learndirect are identified, including the place of in-depth guidance within helpline services, their relationship to wider guidance provision, their framing in relation to national/local, adult/all-age and learning/career dimensions, the synergy of helplines with other forms of technically mediated service delivery, and the implications of helpline work for the professional development of guidance staff. A postscript provides an update on the subsequent development of the service, and especially the growth of Learndirect's web-based service and the ways in which this has impacted on the helpline.

Transformations in Service Delivery

The growth of helplines and other forms of technically mediated service delivery (Web sites, e-mail, etc.) in the career guidance field can be linked to the transformations taking place in patterns of service delivery in other sectors. These sectoral transformations are infectious because they shape the wider expectations of consumers. Increasingly, it seems, consumers want a service to be available when they identify a need for it with minimum delay and minimum effort: they want it *here*, and they want it *now*. This does not mean that they are unwilling to undertake visits to dedicated physical locations where this offers added value, either through face-to-face interaction or through access to physical resources (e.g., in the case of shopping, being able to see and touch particular goods). But their "decision rules" in these respects are becoming more and more discriminating.

Helplines are not new. The origins of the Samaritans service, aimed at individuals in crisis or considering suicide, go back to the 1950s (Varah, 1988). But helplines have grown massively in recent years. The first UK *Directory of Helplines*, issued in 1996 by the Telephone Helplines Association, listed some 800 national, regional and local services that claimed to follow helpline standards for good practice (Rosenfield, 1997) (this figure is reported by the Association to have since risen to around 1,000). Moreover, there has been a huge growth of commercial call centers, which are now one of the fastest-growing employment sectors. It is estimated that by 2005, over 3% of the UK's working population will be employed in over 8,500 call centers (Datamonitor, 2000).

Why has the use of the telephone for service delivery grown so rapidly? There seem to be at least three explanations. One is the much more extensive *availability* of telephones – the proportion of households with home telephones rose from around one-third in 1970 to 95% in 1999/00 (Office for National Statistics, 2001, p. 233) and is now significantly enhanced by the massive growth of mobile phones. Secondly, there is much more sophisticated *support technology* now available for routing calls, diverting them into or out of pre-coded voice response systems, and providing database support for call center staff. A third reason is *cultural change*, linked in particular to the growth of consumerism, and the trend towards a "24-hour society" in which work and other activities are not confined to specified hours.

Also pertinent are the knock-on effects of Web sites and e-mail, which similarly are encouraging providers and consumers to expect new and more immediate forms of service delivery. Hitherto the telephone, the computer, and television have been viewed as separate technologies. But the advent of digital technology and enhanced bandwidth means that these three separate "analogue streams" are now converging into an integrated "digital river" (Cunningham & Fröschl, 1999). The potential implications of this are profound and will be considered towards the end of this paper.

Clearly, the telephone is now being used for a wide range of service provision. At one end of the spectrum are services comprising a menu leading to a series of pre-coded messages, or direct contact with a member of the call center staff who is encouraged to minimize call length and work within a series of prescribed "scripts." At the other end are highly interactive engagements with skilled professionals. Within a helping context, the telephone can be used for a variety of interventions, ranging from information and advice, to support, befriending, and advocacy, to counseling (Rosenfield, 1997). Even deep and long-term counseling work can be carried out over the telephone, not only with individuals, but also with groups (Rosenfield & Smillie, 1998).

Applications in Career Guidance

Changes in service delivery in other sectors are likely to affect the expectations of those who are looking for help with career decisions and transitions. Reardon, Sampson, and Lenz (2000) suggest that such individuals increasingly need to be viewed not as "clients" but as "career shoppers." They may engage in such "shopping" at varied times and places, and often want to preview or try out services before they "buy" or "buy into" them. They are commonly looking for "bargains" and "value," and frequently place limits on the time they are prepared to invest.

Prior to Learndirect, some use had already been made of the telephone in guidance work in the UK. Examples included a national Careerline service operated by the Association of Graduate Careers Advisory Services (Madahar, 2000). Elsewhere, the main early reported applications were in the USA, as part of the concept of "educational brokering" (Heffernan, Macy, & Vickers, 1976), linking adults to learning opportunities. The most ambitious early effort to provide career counseling via telephone was the home-based career education model program located in Rhode Island, aimed particularly at home-based women (Arbeiter, Aslanian, Schmerback, & Brickell, 1978). Other experimental telephone-based services tended similarly to be aimed at groups unable to access face-to-face services because they were home-based, or were based in rural areas, or for other reasons (Roach, Reardon, Alexander, & Cloudman, 1983; Heppner, Johnston, & Brinkhoff, 1988).

More recently, a major development is occurring in New Zealand. Here, a pilot has taken place of a new CareerPoint telephone helpline service to be run by the publicly-funded Career Services as part of its range of services, which also includes 16 career centers and a training and job information Web site. The pilot was based in part on the Learndirect model, though it is more strongly integrated into a comprehensive service, is designed as a "career" rather than a "learning" helpline, and is aimed at people of all ages (Adair, Patten, & Kalafatelis, 2000). Following the pilot, the New Zealand Government has confirmed ongoing funding for the service.

These various services indicate the variety of ways in which the telephone can be used in career guidance delivery. Some of the services have been promoted essentially as information services; others as career counseling services. Some are focused primarily on learning or work; others on career, embracing the two. Some are aimed at young people or adults; others are all-age. Some are separate services based in small call centers; others are integrated in various ways into more broadly-based services. These contrasts identify some of the range of options within which the design of Learndirect was located, and will be revisited as issues later in this paper.

The Evolution of Learndirect

The notion of a national helpline on learning opportunities emerged from the adult education field in the early 1990s. It was initially decided to set up the helpline in a single call center, to be run by Broadcasting Support Services (BSS) and based in Manchester. This was launched in February 1998 as Learning Direct, having been preceded by the launch of the Scottish helpline in August 1997. The inauguration of Learning Direct coincided with the publication of a Government document that also announced the setting up of the University for Industry (UfI) as a major new initiative designed to use new technology to improve learning and skills, and to "connect those who want to learn with ways of doing so" (Department for Education and Employment, 1998a, p. 18). It stated that "Learning Direct will become the UfI information and advice service when the UfI opens for business" (p. 22).

In the consultation process that followed the green paper, some concern was expressed that the impartiality of the service offered by the helpline might be compromised by UfI's role as a learning provider. Although initially conceived primarily as a broker of learning opportunities (Hillman, 1996), it seemed likely that the commercial pressures exerted by its need to become increasingly self-funding would lead in the direction of acting as a provider, in the sense of commissioning and endorsing particular learning packages and having its own registered students. The concern was that this might lead it to exert pressures on the learning line to promote these opportunities in preference to others. Nonetheless, the decision to locate responsibility for running the helpline within UfI went ahead, and in June 1999 the sub-contract held by BSS, along with the relevant database contracts, were novated by DfEE to UfI. Indeed, the relationship between UfI and the helpline was made perceptually more seamless by a decision not only to rebrand Learning Direct as Learndirect, but also to use the same brand name for UfI learning packages.

Current Operation

Extent

Usage of the helpline has expanded rapidly. The initial target for its first year of operation was 250,000 calls; the actual total was 405,000 (Bysshe & Parsons, 1999). In 1999/2000 it took 639,000 calls; the target for 2000/01 was 1.2 million, with plans to expand to a capacity for handling 4 million (Incomes Data Services, 2000). To cater for this expansion, the original 40 "seats" within the call center at Manchester had by the end of 2000 grown to 110 seats, with a further 110 seats at a second call center in Leicester. BSS is also responsible for the 8-seat Learndirect helpline service for Northern Ireland, based in Belfast, which opened in June 2000. The services for Scotland and Wales are managed separately, with the Scottish service being based in Glasgow, and the Welsh service operating from four small helplines based in local careers services. This diversity reflects the growing diversification of guidance policy in the UK post-devolution (Watts, 1999a; 2001). All four national services are, however, marketed as Learndirect, use a single telephone number, and are subject to a four-countries agreement to offer minimum common standards of service.

Distance Counseling

Availability

The opening hours for the helpline are from 9:00 a.m. to 9:00 p.m. Monday to Friday and from 9:00 a.m. to noon on Saturday. The rate of calls is volatile and seems to be very sensitive to marketing campaigns, especially on television. There are also seasonal fluctuations related, for example, to course start dates. Building and maintaining capacity to meet demand and to avoid caller frustration has not been easy. The rate of successful connection has however increased significantly since the inception of the service: from under 50% in the first year to around 94% in early 2000 (monitoring data). The risk of losing out-of-hours calls was noted in the evaluation by Bysshe & Parsons (1999, p. 8). However, it is worth noting that, in a national survey of 250 call centers, two-thirds operated seven days a week, and over one-third operated on a 24-hour basis over the seven days (Incomes Data Services, 2000).

Staffing

The staffing structure of the service has been based on a distinction between Information Advisers who are qualified to National Vocational Qualification (NVQ) Level 2 in Service Support, and Learning Advisers who are qualified to NVQ Level 3 in Guidance. There is a structured progression route for Information Advisers who wish to become Learning Advisers. The staff works in small mixed teams of 12. Between two-thirds and three-quarters of their time is spent on calls; time is also set aside for NVQ study or for investigations into new learning-opportunity developments (Incomes Data Services, 2000, p. 97). There is no "scripting" of calls: staff are viewed as the "jazz players" of the call center world (p. 98).

A further layer of staffing was introduced in May 2000, linked to the introduction of a Learndirect Web site alongside the helpline. The Web site includes not only courses and occupations databases, but also a "Futures" diagnostic package which enables a self-assessment of skills, interests, and values and connects the results to occupational families. Each page of the Web site includes a "call me" button which generates a telephone call from a Learndirect adviser. To deal with such calls, a new small team of Lifelong Learning Advisers has been set up, who are expected to hold, or be working towards, a Level 4 NVQ in Guidance.

This means that there are now three levels of advisers: Information Advisers dealing with straightforward "information" requests; Learning Advisers dealing with enquiries requiring "advice"; and Lifelong Learning Advisers dealing with enquiries requiring "advice and guidance" – a term selected to represent a midway position between "advice" and "guidance." The structure thus mirrors the distinctions between "information," "advice," and "guidance," which have been the basis of recent adult guidance policy (Department for Education and Employment, 1998b). Implicitly, these levels could lead to a fourth level – full "guidance" – which the service does not claim to offer. It is anticipated that the expansion of the Web site will make it easier to answer straightforward information enquiries, and that this will mean that the helpline "will increasingly deal with a higher proportion of more complex calls from people requiring more detailed advice" (Incomes Data Services, 2000, p. 98).

Users

Part of the policy rationale for the service was the hope that it would reach non-traditional learners. The first-year evaluation by Bysshe and Parsons (1999) found that only 8% of callers had no or very low levels of qualification, compared with 36% qualified at first-degree level or above. Over half of users are aged 18-35; intriguingly, a further 4% are aged 17 or under – and therefore strictly outside the service's client group (Wiseman & Parry, 2000, p. 16). In terms of gender, a majority (60%) of callers are women (*ibid*, p.13): this is a common finding among helplines – the figure for CareerPoint in New Zealand was identical (Adair, Patten, & Kalafatelis, 2000, p. 9).

User ratings of the service have been high. Of the respondents in customer feedback surveys, 93% agreed that the overall quality of the service had been good, and 92% that they would recommend it to others. Satisfaction levels on a five-point scale for a variety of specified criteria ranged from 4.00 to 4.53 (Wiseman & Parry, 2000, pp. 55, 58).

In terms of effects, a short-term follow-up survey found that the proportion of callers participating in full- or part-time education and training had more than doubled. Of the 9% of users who had moved from being unemployed or unwaged to paid work, nearly half attributed the change to the helpline to "a great" or at least "some" extent. In addition, 73% indicated that it had raised their awareness of relevant education/training opportunities, 57%

that it had contributed to their career planning, and 40% that it had improved their self-confidence (Bysshe & Parsons, 2000, pp. 52-55).

Issues

In-depth guidance

The Learndirect service has clearly demonstrated the potential of the telephone for delivering career information and guidance. Between its inception in February 1998 and the end of 2000, it had received and responded to 2.4 million calls. This is a very high level of penetration for a single service.

Learndirect does not claim, and indeed has firmly resisted claiming, to offer in-depth "guidance." With the appointment of Lifelong Learning Advisers, though, it has moved a significant step further in this direction. Professional reservations about the feasibility of offering in-depth guidance over the telephone are refuted by the examples cited earlier of successful practice elsewhere.

The real reason for the current restriction of Learndirect in relation to in-depth guidance is not its feasibility, but the relatively low priority attached to it in policy terms. The two-level model, which has been the basis of Government policy on adult guidance since the mid-1990s, has been based on public funding for information and brief advice. It has been signposted as a service that is free and accessible to all, with in-depth guidance available free to specified groups, especially the unemployed, but not "universally supported out of public funds" for the majority of adults in employment (Department for Education and Employment, 1998b, p. 4). This policy is based on the perceived need to control public expenditure. The unit costs of in-depth guidance are relatively high because it is so labor-intensive.

From this perspective, the restrictions on in-depth guidance in the Learndirect service are based on public-funding restrictions and the difficulties of introducing fee-charging within a telephone service of this kind. Almost all helplines and call center services are free to the user or are part of a wider membership subscription package: customers are not accustomed to paying directly for such services. If to this is added the wider difficulties experienced in developing a market in guidance based on fee-charging (Watts, 1999b), it explains why Learndirect has not moved further down this road. Significantly, the web-based "Futures" package to which the role of Lifelong Learning Advisers is linked *is* fee-charged: it is encrypted, and access to it is offered by Learndirect as a costed program. Take-up to date has been limited, so conclusions about its role in a broader guidance offer are probably premature. Helpline advisers have been making it available free of charge on a trial basis, and it can also be used free of charge within UfI learning centres. In addition, the Department for Education and Employment (DfEE) have made it available free for a six-month period to members of Information, Advice and Guidance for Adults (IAGA) Partnerships to explore whether such an arrangement should be made permanent, in the interests of equity of access. In light of all this, it seems likely that the rationale for establishing "Futures" as a costed learning program may be open to review, along perhaps with the future development of in-depth guidance within the Learndirect service.

Integration

The wider relationship of Learndirect to IAGA Partnerships also seems worthy of review. As noted earlier, the original plans for the "learning line" envisaged it being linked closely to Local Information Network (LINs). These plans were dropped and the helpline was implemented on a stand-alone contractual basis, largely because of the delays in setting up the LINs. Now the IAGA Partnerships have belatedly been set up, effectively replacing the LINs, with the emphasis shifted from collection and dissemination of information to delivery of information, advice and guidance services. The DfEE specification for the partnerships proscribed the use of DfEE funding for local helplines or information collection because this would duplicate the responsibility of Learndirect. It stated, however, that the partnerships and the Learndirect helpline "must agree a protocol to ensure that effective client referral systems exist between them" (DfEE, 2000, para.18).

The protocol agreed at national level during 2000 stated that Learndirect advisers would refer callers "who have more in depth local IAG needs" to the appropriate local partnership. Each partnership would determine whether it wished referrals to be routed directly to the most appropriate local IAGA service provider to book an appointment, or whether it wanted them to go via a local co-ordinator who would route them appropriately at local level. The process is however rather cumbersome, and it seems likely that some referrals get lost simply because of delays and communication problems.

This issue is an important one, because Learndirect has the potential to become not only a strong delivery vehicle in its own right but also a powerful diagnostic portal into wider career information and guidance services. The first-year evaluation found that only 7-8% of callers had been referred to a local careers or guidance service. It noted that, while it is clear that in-depth guidance "is not an essential prerequisite of effective choice for all adults ... concerns rightly exist about ensuring that, at the least, appropriate individuals are aware of the availability of guidance to enable them to more thoroughly explore their ideas and, at best, that individuals' guidance needs are effectively diagnosed" (Bysshe & Parsons, 1999, pp.56, 73-74). The diagnostic role of Learndirect could in principle be similar in some respects to the triage role of NHS Direct within the National Health Service. But to implement this would require a more comprehensive guidance infrastructure than exists at present, smoother communication channels within this infrastructure (e.g. booking callers direct into face-to-face interviews or group sessions), and clearer referral rules supported by stronger diagnostic tools. For the present, Information Advisers and Learning Advisers working with someone who seems to require more in-depth guidance have discretion to refer them in any of three directions: to a Lifelong Learning Adviser, to the "Futures" programme, or to their local IAGA Partnership.

The reality is that currently the Learndirect helpline is not housed exclusively or even predominantly within a policy frame focused on the delivery of career information and guidance. In policy terms, it is also linked to at least two other major concerns: extending take-up of learning, and extending take-up of UfI learning packages. None of the three are mutually exclusive, and it may at times be politically useful to link them together: indeed, it could be argued that it is precisely their conflation that has secured the public funding for the helpline. But operationally they weight the service in different directions. If, for example, access to learning is prioritised, this would tend to encourage maximising "direct-route" entry to learning programmes: from this perspective, low levels of referrals to in-depth guidance services might be regarded as an appropriate performance measure. If, on the other hand, greater priority is attached to encouraging individuals to review their career interests, talents and career direction in some depth before committing themselves to a particular programme, then the appropriate performance measure would be *high* levels of such referrals.

Impartiality

The issue of the promotion of UfI learning packages adds a further complication. As noted earlier, concern was expressed during the consultations that preceded the setting-up of the helpline about the risk that this would compromise the impartiality of the service. From UfI's perspective as a learning provider, the issue is whether it believes that providing an impartial service will in the end result in enrolments from more learners and more motivated learners than a more narrowly-based marketing strategy. This is not a unique dilemma: it is faced by all learning providers. The UfI faces the issue in a particularly stark and visible way.

In practice, the accreditation to the Guidance Council quality standards by the Guidance Accreditation Board (GAB) provides external endorsement of the impartiality of the information and advice that is offered. The culture of the Learndirect callcentres is strongly learner-centred; the level of take-up of Learndirect courses by callers is recorded in monitoring reports – in 1999/2000 it represented 4% of callers (Wiseman & Parry, 2000, p.61) – but is not used as a performance measure.

It is also worth noting that the case with which the service can be accessed makes it very transparent. "Mystery callers" are not confined to formal evaluations (or, indeed, to GAB accreditation processes, which include "mystery shoppers"): learning providers concerned that they are receiving due mention can test the service to see whether this is the case – and not infrequently do so. Since the helpline is a separate DfEE contract based on the principle of impartiality, any serious evidence that this is being infringed could imperil the contract.

Nonetheless, the use of the name Learndirect to brand both the impartial helpline service and the UfI's own learning provision may confuse the perceived impartiality of the service in the eyes of some potential and actual callers. Moreover, the principal marketing campaigns – based, in particular, around a "Walks of Life" television advertisement – have tended to blur the distinctions between guidance, learning, and UfI learning provision. It also seems possible that confusion about impartiality has limited the number of "trails" which the BBC has provided from its mainstream programmes. Concerns have been expressed by BBC staff that such trails may be seen as favouring one learning provider over others.

Framing

National v. local. The current structure of the Learndirect service determines the way in which it is framed in at least three key respects. The first is the extent to which the service is offered at national or at local level. The medical helpline NHS Direct, for example, is a national service, operated locally. Calls are routed to the local call center, though they are passed elsewhere when lines are busy. Part of the rationale for this is the notion that, in time, it might become the "gateway" to all local health services (McLennan, 1999). Elsewhere in the UK, however, the notion is that the helpline should operate at a national level, and that local information should be offered on a face-to-face basis. This can result in some loss of quality: one of the areas of concern identified in the first-year evaluation was "lack of local knowledge, including broad understanding of geography and detailed understanding of local learning and guidance provision, networks and referral agencies, and transport" (Bysshe & Parsons, 1999, p.18). Against this needs to be set the consistency of service and adviser training offered by relatively large-scale operation.

Adults v. all-age. The second is the extent to which the service is confined to adults or might be extended to young people too. The Learndirect service was formally designated as being for adults (aged over 18), though it has attracted some younger users. There is currently much discussion about developing a Connexions Direct service as part of the new Connexions Service for young people. A pilot is due to start in the North-East in autumn 2001. Connexions Direct is designed to "use call centre and web technology to help Connexions reach out effectively to all young people," and "will be an integral part of local Connexions provision, offering a complementary tier of service delivery" (Connexions Web site, www.connexions.gov.uk, April 2001). A key issue here, again, is whether the helpline will be national or local: "some information and advice can be offered effectively through Web sites and helplines at national level, but some will have more credibility if it is grounded in local knowledge" (Offer & Watts, 2000). In addition, it could be totally separate from Learndirect, or integrated with it. The CareerPoint helpline service in New Zealand is deliberately all-age, and indeed 26% of callers in its pilot were aged under 20 (Adair, Patten, & Kalafatelis, 2000, p. 41). In the UK, decisions on this may well be linked to wider policies on guidance provision: in Scotland and Wales, the current policy is to encourage "vertical" integration of careers services on an all-age basis, whereas in England it favors "horizontal" integration of guidance services for young people (personal and social as well as related to learning and work) (Watts, 1999a; 2001).

Learning v. career. This leads to the third framing issue: the extent to which the service focuses on "learning" or on "career" (in either a broad or narrow sense). The focus of Learndirect has been on "learning." The first-year evaluation report found that the emphasis of the information was clearly vocational; it also found that the service was better at dealing with learning enquiries than with enquiries about careers and other opportunities (Bysshe & Parsons, 1999, pp. 38, 73). Later customer feedback surveys indicated that expectations of the service tended to be focused around "courses," and that levels of satisfaction were higher in this area than in more job-related areas (Wiseman & Parry, 2000, pp. 28, 33). A new Employment Service Direct helpline was launched in January 1999 to pick up job-related enquiries. Calls are connected to one of over 100 Employment Service teams set up across the country to deliver the service. This reflects the operational separation of the Employment Service from the Department for Education and Employment. In New Zealand, on the other hand, the CareerPoint service is focused on "career" and brings together both "learning" and "work." A customer satisfaction survey of its pilot found that 73% of users contacted the service "to find out what to steps to take to pursue a particular career," 65% "to find out what training courses are offered," 38% to "look to changes of jobs or careers," and 36% "to find out about how to choose a career" (BRC Marketing and Social Research, 2001). A new helpline for young people launched in March 2001 by Careers Management Ltd. in advance of Connexions Direct has similarly adopted the title "Careerline." It seems likely, however, that Connexions Direct itself will be much more broadly based, covering personal and social as well as educational and vocational issues. The "labeling" of a service and the way in which it is promoted strongly determine the kinds of calls it receives.

Technological synergy

The Learndirect helpline and Web site are managed separately: the former by BSS; the latter by Citizen Connect. This has restricted the extent to which the two services have been planned in an integrated way, though the BSS contract includes providing support for the "Futures" program within the Web site. There are opportunities for increased synergy. For example, a user of the CV section of "Futures" could ring a telephone adviser, who could then bring up on their screen the caller's work to date and talk it through with them. Conversely, more telephone callers could be encouraged to use the Web site and be supported in doing so. At present, only 7% of respondents in customer feedback surveys indicate that they have even visited the site (Wiseman & Parry, 2000, p.57).

A related issue is the use of e-mail. This is currently limited to users of the "Futures" program who are invited to use e-mail at particular points, notably the CV-building section. The rule is that the client selects the medium: if they enquire via by e-mail, they are responded to via e-mail. The potential for extending use of e-mail is considerable. Currently, printed provision is sent to around one-third of callers by postal mail (Wiseman & Parry, 2000, p. 9). As domestic usage of e-mail grows, it should be easy after calls to send off this information routinely and immediately as attachments, so reducing the dangers of oral miscommunication and formalizing the information for ongoing reference. Greater use of e-mail might also make it possible to sustain contact with a particular adviser over a period of time through a mixture of synchronous (telephone) and asynchronous (e-mail) communications. At present, 15% of users are repeat callers (p. 3).

The current limited synergy between telephone and Web-based services reflects what is happening in call centers more generally. A survey by Incomes Data Services (2000) found that only a small proportion of call centers could be regarded as fully "web-integrated," although a large number were planning to move in this direction. Call centers are now predicted to evolve into multi-media "contact centers," capable of dealing not only with telephone calls, but also with contacts via e-mail, the Web, and interactive digital television.

The concept of iterative contact with Learndirect through flexible usage of the telephone, Web site and e-mail, linked selectively with local face-to-face facilities, opens up new opportunities for the delivery of career information and guidance. It means that individuals can access help in the form in which they feel comfortable. Some feel comfortable visiting a careers centre; some do not. Some are more comfortable on the telephone, or on e-mail; some are not. Clearer models, based on users' experiences, regarding the strengths and weaknesses of the different media, and ways in which they can be effectively combined, could provide a stronger basis for planning coherent service delivery.

A further dimension could be added to this by the likely move towards ready domestic access to videophones (Kraut & Fish, 1997) or interactive television. Already, desktop videoconferencing is growing, and experiments have taken place in its use for guidance as well as selection interviewing (Oborne, Chen, & Slater, 2001). An evaluation of an experiment involving audioconferencing (in which adviser and students could talk to one another and share career guidance software) and videoconferencing (where they could also see one another) found that, although videoconferencing was felt to be useful for establishing rapport in the early stages of an interview, it was not felt to be significantly more successful than audioconferencing during the part of the interview where the focus was on "application sharing" (discussion of an interest profile and job suggestions, represented in the shared software). Indeed, it was felt that it could even be a distraction here. Both, however, were considered more satisfactory than the use of the telephone on its own (Closs & Miller, 1997). This was a limited experiment, and the evidence should not be regarded as being in any way definitive. But the addition of video links and/or synchronised access to web-based resources seem likely to add significantly to the potential of the telephone.

Professional development of guidance staff

A final issue to be addressed is implications for the training and career progression paths of career guidance staff. We have noted that the present Learndirect structure of Information Advisers, Learning Advisers and Lifelong Learning Advisers offers both differentiation of skill levels and a potential route for career progression. Added to the lack of "scripting" of calls, this has enabled Learndirect to avoid some of the problems, experienced by many call centers, of low staff morale and high turnover (Incomes Data Services, 2000; Trades Union Congress, 2001). Levels of staff retention are reported to be much higher than in most call centers.

An interesting issue is whether telephone guidance should be viewed as a distinctive specialization within the guidance field or as one among many areas of application for generic staff. This is linked to the question of whether or not it is helpful for advisers to have ongoing experience of face-to-face guidance work alongside their telephone work. Some Learndirect staff combine a couple of evening shifts with a traditional careers adviser job in the daytime (Incomes Data Services, 2000, p. 96); in Belfast, some of the helpline staff do face-to-face work within the Educational Guidance Service for adults where the helpline is based. Further research is needed to assess how far such face-to-face involvement improves the quality of their work on the helpline. The same issue arises in, for example, the case of NHS Direct, where current policy on staff rotation varies between local sites. Some favor whole-time appointments; others favor split posts and rotational schemes with primary or secondary care services in order to maintain clinical competencies (McLennan, 1999). In the guidance field, it is possible that staying too long on exclusively telephone work might result in some atrophy of generic guidance skills – for example, interpreting visual signals, and building rapport.

A related issue is whether some experience of face-to-face work should be required in the training of helpline advisers. Until recently, such experience was required in order to gain evidence for the NVQ Level 3 (this is no longer the case). There is anecdotal evidence that some of the Learndirect advisers found this daunting: they felt exposed by not being able to refer invisibly to the database and felt safer and more in control in the call center environment. This could, however, be regarded as strengthening the case for such experience. Conversely, it has been argued in the case of counseling that the lack of visual evidence in the audio mode prevents counselors from making judgments based on appearance and refines their listening skills, suggesting that the use of audio counseling in generic training programs would be beneficial (Day & Schneider, 2000). The same case could be made in relation to guidance.

A final question regarding professional development is whether it is essential for advisers to work in the call center or whether they could work effectively from home. A survey of call centers by Huws and Denbigh (1999) found that although only 4% were currently employing home workers, a further 42% expected to do so in the future (p. 41). Some Learndirect advisers are interested in becoming home-based teleworkers, for personal reasons. If such an option is offered, should it be offered only to people who have already worked in the call center or to new recruits as well? Could Learndirect in due course become a virtual call center?

Conclusion

The development of the Learndirect helpline service has demonstrated the potential of the telephone for delivering personalized career information and advice on a massive scale. Telephone guidance sits somewhere between face-to-face guidance and web-based guidance: it combines the synchronous interactivity of face-to-face work with the "at a distance" accessibility of Web-based work. Its potential has been underutilized in many countries to date. The example of Learndirect shows what can be achieved and some of the issues that need to be addressed.

The case-study of Learndirect also indicates the extent to which public-policy issues shape decision-making in relation to guidance services in general, but particularly so in relation to major initiatives in technically mediated service delivery (cf. Watts, 1993). The level of public investment required is so substantial, and the decisions required have to be so clear-cut, that the underlying economic and political issues are more manifest than they often are in relation to direct human services. The constraints imposed by the contractual structure of the Learndirect helpline has constrained its capacity for total service redesign – in comparison, for example, with NHS Direct or, indeed, the New Zealand CareerPoint service. On the other hand, the links with a high-profile Government initiative like the University for Industry have arguably made it possible to command much more substantial resources than would otherwise have been the case. It is this that has made it possible to demonstrate – more clearly than hitherto – the potential of helplines in the career guidance field.

Postscript

The paper (Watts & Dent, 2002) on which the article above was based was published in February 2002. Since then, the service has continued to flourish, but significant changes have taken place in the balance and relationship between Learndirect's helpline and its Web-based service. By late 2006 the number of calls to the helpline had expanded to over 8 million. The annual level of usage had however reduced from a peak of 1.3 million to around 800,000 in 2005/06. Meanwhile, the number of sessions on the Web site had expanded from a quarter of a million in its first 8 months (2000/01) to 8.8 million in 2005/06 (a session is defined not just as a 'hit' but as including a completed information search). Around one in seven of those ringing on the helpline have now previously used the Web site.

This has altered the nature of the calls received. Whereas in the early years of the service most of the calls were for information and advice, a much higher proportion now require in-depth guidance. This has been recognized by the Government, which has funded a pilot scheme to extend Learndirect's offer of in-depth guidance, particularly to low-skilled workers and women returning to the labor market. Accordingly, the balance of staff in the call centers has changed, with a higher proportion of Lifelong Learning Advisers. An evaluation of the pilot concluded that it had demonstrated both the demand for telephone guidance, and that it can be – and in many cases is – as good as the best face-to-face practice (Page *et al.*, 2007).

Another significant development has been a variable languages service. The helpline service is now available not just in English and Welsh, but also in Farsi, French, Gujerati, Polish, Punjabi, Somali, Sylheti and Urdu.

Finally, progress has been made in using monitoring data to improve the cost-efficiency of the service (Watts & Dent, 2006). One of the benefits of a centralized service with substantial critical mass in terms of resources is that it is able to addressing 'productivity' issues (in terms of clients benefits from resources committed) more systematically than smaller services can.

References

Adair, C., Patten, D., & Kalafatelis, E. (2000). *CareerPoint pilot evaluation.* Wellington, New Zealand: Career Services (mimeo).

Arbeiter, S., Aslanian, C., Schmerback, F., & Brickell, H. (1978). *Telephone counseling for home-based adults.* New York: College Entrance Examination Board.

BRC Marketing and Social Research. (2001). *CareerPoint customer satisfaction survey.* Wellington, New Zealand: BRC Marketing and Social Research.

Bysshe, S., & Parsons, D. (1999). *Evaluation on learning direct.* Research Report RR132. London: Department for Education and Employment.

Closs, S. J., & Miller, I. M. (1997). *Careers guidance at a distance: An evaluation of desktop video conferencing technology.* London: Department for Education and Employment.

Cunningham, P., & Fröschl, F. (1999). *Electronic business revolution.* Berlin, Germany: Springer.

Datamonitor. (2000). *Call centres in EMEA.* London: Datamonitor.

Day, S. X., & Schneider, P. (2000). The subjective experiences of therapists in face-to-face, video, and audio sessions. In J. W. Bloom & G. R. Walz (Eds), *Cybercounseling and cyberlearning:Strategies and resources for the millennium.* Alexandria, VA: American Counseling Association/ CAPS, Inc.

Department for Education and Employment. (1998a). *The learning age: A renaissance for a new Britain.* Cmd. 3790. London: Stationery Office.

Department for Education and Employment. (1998b). *Local information, advice and guidance for adults in England – Towards a national framework.* London: DfEE.

Department for Education and Employment. (2000). *Local information, advice and guidance services for adults: Specification for IAG partnerships 2000-2001.* London: DfEE (mimeo).

Heffernan, J., Macy, F. U., & Vickers, D. F. (1976). *Educational brokering: A new service for adult learners.* Syracuse, NY: National Center for Educational Brokering.

Heppner, M. J., Johnston, J. A., & Brinkhoff, J. (1988). Creating a career hotline for rural residents. *Journal of Counseling and Development, 66*(7), 340-341.

Hillman, J. (1996). *University for Industry: Creating a national learning network.* London: Institute for Public Policy Research.

Huws, U., & Denbigh, A. (1999). *Virtually there – the evolution of call centres.* London: Mitel (mimeo).

Incomes Data Services. (2000). *Pay and conditions in call centres 2000.* London: IDS.

Kraut, R. E., & Fish, R. S. (1997). Prospects for videophony. In K. E. Finn, A. J. Sellen, & S. B. Wilbur (Eds), *Video-mediated communication,* (pp. 541-561). Mahwah, NJ: Erlbaum.

Madahar, L. (2000). Services to graduates. *Phoenix, 94,* 6-7.

McLennan, N. (1999). NHS Direct: here and now. *Archives of Disease in Childhood, 81,* 376-378.

Oborne, D. J., Chen, M., & Slater, F. W. (2001). *Remote multi media interviewing (RMI): Guidelines for interviewers and interviewees using desk top video conferencing (DVC).* Swansea, UK: University of Wales Swansea (mimeo).

Offer, M., & Watts, A. G. (2000). *The use of information and communications technologies in the Connexions service.* CRAC/NICEC Conference Briefing. Cambridge, UK: Careers Research and Advisory Centre.

Page, R., Newton, B., Hawthorn, R., Hunt, W. & Hillage, J. (2007). *An evaluation of UfI/Learndirect telephone guidance trial.* Research Report RR833. London: Department for Education and Skills.

Reardon, R. C., Sampson, J. P., & Lenz, J. G. (2000). Career assessment in a time of changing roles, relationships, and context. *Journal of Career Assessment, 8*(4), 351-359.

Roach, D., Reardon, R., Alexander, J., & Cloudman, D. (1983). Career counseling by telephone. *Journal of College Student Personnel*, 24, 71-76.

Rosenfield, M. (1997). *Counseling by telephone.* London: Sage.

Rosenfield, M., & Smillie, E. (1998). Group counseling by telephone. *British Journal of Guidance and Counseling, 26*(1), 11-19.

Trades Union Congress. (2001). *It's your call.* London: TUC.

Varah, C. (Ed.). (1988). *The Samaritans: Befriending the suicidal* (Rev. ed.). London: Constable.

Watts, A. G. (1993). The politics and economics of computer-aided careers guidance systems. *British Journal of Guidance and Counseling, 21*(2), 175-188.

Watts, A. G. (1999a). *Home internationals: Adult guidance policy developments in Britain and Ireland.* CRAC/NICEC Conference Briefing. Cambridge, UK: Careers Research and Advisory Centre.

Watts, A. G. (1999b). *Reshaping career development for the 21st century.* CeGS Occasional Paper. Derby, UK: Centre for Guidance Studies, University of Derby.

Watts, A. G. (2001). Career guidance and social exclusion: A cautionary tale. British Journal of Guidance and Counseling, 29(2), 157-176.

Watts, A. G. & Dent, G. (2002). 'Let your fingers do the walking': the use of telephone helplines in career information and guidance. *British Journal of Guidance and Counselling, 30*(1), 17-35.

Watts, A. G. & Dent, G. (2006). The 'P' word: productivity in the delivery of career guidance services. *British Journal of Guidance and Counselling, 34*(2), 177-189.

Wiseman, J., & Parry, E. (2000). *UfI Ltd customer feedback: Summary report, October 1999 – September 2000.* Birmingham, UK: BMG (mimeo).

Tony Watts is a self-employed consultant, based in Cambridge, England. He was for many years Director of the National Institute for Careers Education and Counselling, and remains a Fellow. He is also Visiting Professor at the University of Derby and at Canterbury Christ Church University.

Gareth Dent is Head of Advice Services at Ufi, the educational charity responsible for learndirect in the UK. A labour market economist by training, he joined Ufi at launch from the Civil Service, where he was responsible for adult guidance policy.

APPENDIX B

The ReadyMinds Story: Transforming a Vision into a Reality... And What Comes Next?

Randy M. Miller

The Story Behind the Creation of a Distance Counseling Company

Today, ReadyMinds is the most prominent distance career counseling and training company in the United States, and it has taken a leading role in advancing the field of counseling in the online technology sector. ReadyMinds, however, was not founded as an online "dotcom" company. The initial model was built on traditional face-to-face counselor/client relationships. With an entrepreneurial methodology and the advent of the Internet, new doors were opened, and an entirely new model evolved.

This "epilogue" is intended as a narrative summary designed to show you the personal, business, and counseling insights that led to the creation of Ready & Motivated Minds (ReadyMinds). As the Founder and CEO of ReadyMinds, I believe the company was born largely out of my own experiences; and it is these fibers, woven together, that led me to create a private, for-profit company dedicated to counseling, training, and coaching. ReadyMinds came about as a way to fulfill my need to nurture the passion of others and to help people identify their potential, harness their strengths, and find courage in their decision making. This is what others had done for me. The culmination of this mission, in my mind, was helping others embark upon and embrace career opportunities that would provide not just a job, but a fulfillment of their individual skills, talents, and personal vision. Since the inception of ReadyMinds seven and a half years ago, I have been asked on several occasions to share the ReadyMinds story. Namely, where did the idea to start a counseling "business" come from, and did I start out in the field as a counselor?

Along with the personal inquiries, there are many questions about the field of Distance Career Counseling. "What exactly is it?" Or, "I've heard of it, how does it work?" "How effective is it?" "How can I find out more?"

I begin to tell the story and people say, "Wow, what a great idea. I wish I would have had that when I was in school," or "If only I'd known about this when I was looking for a job." As someone interested or involved in this field, you know that it is through this sharing of your experiences as a counselor, coach, teacher, or mentor that you not only light the way for others, but become more enlightened yourself. It is these stories, yours and mine, that consistently reinforce the importance of mentoring, coaching, and counseling.

At some point in life, most of us ponder a career move or change, but often have trouble figuring out what it is we want or are best suited to do. For some, this may mean having few if any ideas about what they like to do. For others, there are vague notions of a career that seems interesting; but armed with little or no information on the specifics of the day-to-day job, it is tough to make a decision on whether or not it would be a good fit. In some cases, focusing on just one career option seems difficult because there are many that seem exciting. For some, this process happens once in their life, while for others, it is a continual process. More often than not, there is a desire to share these thoughts with someone—other than our friends, parents, spouses or partners—who could provide us with guidance (i.e., unbiased opinions). If you have found yourself in the field of counseling or training as a profession, you may have experienced these decision-making dynamics yourself, and most certainly, you work with individuals every day who are asking themselves what their next move will be. As you know, finding an answer to this question is part of a process that requires time, energy, introspection, and honesty. The questions you may ask yourself if you have forayed into the "distance" space are, "Can we really help people using 21st century technology?" "Can I guide someone through this exploration without ever seeing them?" "If so, how?"

Given the relative newness of the field of Distance Counseling/coaching, it is not unusual to question the validity of what you are doing. Isn't the foundation of quality counseling or coaching still a one-on-one relationship? Sure, and to think otherwise would be denying the true essence of counseling and/or coaching… helping people. The word distance is slightly misleading. Yes, there may be a physical distance between the counselor/coach and the client, but technology has the ability to do more than bridge that distance. It can create new pathways for both giving and receiving information and often establishes a meaningful and intimate counselor/client relationship as many of the physiological barriers that may inhibit truly open communication are removed.

As information technology becomes embedded in our society, working in a Web-based environment becomes the norm, not the exception. With this technology come certain expectations about relationships and new norms of interaction—ones that didn't exist 20 years ago. The growing familiarity and normalcy of distance interactions - whether with a bank, a work colleague, or a potential date - is increasingly making Distance Counseling the norm, not the exception. The availability of counseling in an online platform has and will continue to attract individuals who may have never considered any type of counseling or coaching in a traditional face-to-face environment. But, because it is online in an environment they are comfortable in, barriers or preconceived notions about counseling become less daunting and encourage participation.

Here are some comments from ReadyMinds Distance Counseling clients quoted with their permission:

Anne P., Job Seeker /Alumna, Harvard University
"I was very satisfied with the ReadyMinds Program. I loved the flexibility of being able to talk with my ReadyMinds Counselor when it was convenient for me. ReadyMinds worked around my rigid work schedule. It was comforting to know that I didn't need to take my lunch hour and talk quietly at my previous job about job searching for something new! For my friends or colleagues who are struggling (even in their late 20's) with what they want to do for a career, this might be just what they need to get them thinking about their options."

Marina G., Job Seeker / Alumna, Pace University
"During our sessions, my counselor disclosed many options to me - alternatives that I had not realized I had. Telecounseling made me feel comfortable enough to reveal any questions or doubts that I was experiencing. It also made me realize that my personal interests and my career did not have to be mutually exclusive. Most importantly, I felt as though my counselor was genuinely interested in my career goals. Insight

Into U was the most rewarding phase of the ReadyMinds Program. The "to do" list contained all of the research I needed to do in my personal situation. Each phase of the ReadyMinds Program brought me a step closer to my future career success. I want to thank my counselor from the bottom of my heart for pointing me into the right direction when I needed it the most. I just accepted a job and at this point in my life, I honestly cannot be happier. I will forever be grateful."

Lashawndra P., Job Seeker/Graduate Student, UNC - Chapel Hill
"I think the program was very good. I think it is especially good for someone who can't meet during traditional office hours. I spoke with my counselor at times when school was closed. I also feel that the program did very well helping me, a graduate student, looking to transition out of the academy. I felt comfortable with my counselor and with the advice and suggestions she gave me. The program that you offer is stellar. The feedback that you provided through Insight Into U™ and appropriate website links were great too. Overall, this program is really great and I would highly recommend it to graduate students and undergraduates."

Michael E., Graduate Student, Fordham University
"I was impressed with my counselor's knowledge of me after only one conversation. This knowledge led to very effective recommendations. Her knowledge of the interview process and the process in which I build relationships with potential employers was tremendously helpful. Her sincerity and caring was greatly appreciated. The ReadyMinds Program itself would be an asset to anyone looking to enhance his/her career development."

Jose L., Career Changer/Alumnus, Marien Ngouabi University,
Congo/ Brazzaville
"The ReadyMinds Program helped me gain a sense of FOCUS. For the first time, I did an exhaustive inventory of my interests, skills, and marketability and came up with a game plan for the future. The Quality is GREAT!!! I think you should expand your programs to others coming to America from countries where there is no structure for career planning and/or counseling. Many of them feel lost and could also benefit from your services...Thank you again."

Thomas K., Career Changer, Pace University
"Having personal contact with one particular counselor for a relatively

long period of time forced me to do the work that I wasn't motivated to do while working by myself. Learning to communicate the things I wanted to do, as opposed to merely thinking about them, helped me break through to new insights. We used the internet in a more structured way than I ever had before. I am 33. I can only imagine how this would have revolutionized my life when I was 18, or 21, etc. This program could really change the life of a young man or woman! I have just been offered a position to teach, and now I feel confident enough about what I want to go ahead and throw myself into this fully. Thanks for all your help!"

Sana S., Sophomore, Boston University
"ReadyMinds is a cleverly designed service that assists people of multifarious backgrounds by fulfilling their needs and wants on a personal, social, and professional level. As a business major at Boston University's School of Management, I found the one-on-one counseling sessions to be productive as my counselor understood my concerns about life during and after college. After listening to me and studying my answers for various surveys, she offered constructive feedback on how to seek and enhance the chances of attaining an internship and landing a job of my preference after graduation. With the friendly staff, there is always someone available 24/7 via email to answer my questions and track my academic and professional progress. I think any person with questions and a creative mind is an ideal candidate - it is just a matter of discovering your hidden talents. It is a program that cannot be outdated, because the possibilities in life are endless and we as individuals hold the power in our hands to mold our future."

Whether you are pro or con distance or online methods, there is mounting anecdotal evidence that certain technology-supported counseling and coaching programs are providing successful outcomes for thousands of people.

As you'll learn in this chapter, neither the field, nor its leading company, ReadyMinds, were born overnight. ReadyMinds cannot be characterized as a dot-com success story. The company started out in prime New York office space where it was envisioned that clients would come in, meet privately with counselors, and begin their journey to find the school, career, or personal niche that was best for them. As a "bricks and mortar" operation, the company would primarily cater to people in the New York City Metropolitan area and in a city of ten million people. This wasn't such a bad thing. But, was it as good as it could get, if there were geographic constraints? What was the true mission of the company? It was in contemplating these questions and many others, that the ReadyMinds approach to the field of Distance Career Counseling found its genesis.

ReadyMinds toiled for three years, without accepting revenue or servicing clients, earnestly building its program, content, services, training, and intellectual assets. And, yes, as you may have surmised by now, the idea was germinating way before then.

If you are in the counseling field already, or thinking about becoming a counselor or coach, you'll find that a key element in your work is or will be discovering a person's "history." What is their "story"? Where did they come from? How did they get to where they are today? What is their academic background? What is their family situation? Who are their peers of influence? As you study the field of Distance Counseling, and in some cases, the evolution of ReadyMinds within the distance field, it might be helpful for you to get to know RMM, Randy Michael Miller, the "business" guy, the non-official counselor, the Founder and CEO, and the man. What was my journey? What role did my experiences, family, peers, struggles, and triumphs play in setting the course of my career? As trained counselors, these are the things you learn as part of any professional counselor-client relationship. Learning a client's story is a significant mode of discovery and is often what drives us to be part of this wonderful, exciting counseling profession. This is my personal story and the story of what is now ReadyMinds, the Company—shared "via distance" with you now.

The month is September. The year, 1985. The Place, Kingston, Rhode Island, home of the University of Rhode Island. Little did I know as I stood gazing at the pristine buildings of the URI quad that standing here on this day was the beginning of a journey that would take me down a path I never imagined, and set me on course to help many others that would follow in my footsteps.

The crisp, clear fall day matched the exuberance I felt as a young, freshman student, born and raised in Philadelphia, Pennsylvania, who suddenly finds himself in a new world. Just being here was somewhat of a miracle. My senior year of high school turned out to be a turning point in my life. No, it wasn't acne, a prom date disaster, or problems in school. It was a neurological disease called Guillain-Barré Syndrome.

It came out of nowhere. Suddenly, I started having trouble getting up from the basic squat position, had trouble walking up stairs at home. Assuming it was just fatigue, I used the lockers at school and stair railings at home as support. I was 18 and invincible—whatever this was would disappear as quickly as it had come. It didn't.

For eight weeks I lay in a hospital bed as numerous doctors examined every nerve in my body, but offered no diagnosis. After much deliberation, the doctors performed a spinal tap... not a procedure I would recommend, but it did yield a diagnosis: Guillain-Barré Syndrome, a disease that affects one of every 100,000 people. Also known as GBS, it is a debilitating disease that affects the central nervous system.

Once diagnosed, I immediately began physical therapy in the hospital to rebuild my muscles and regain control over my motor functions. Four to six weeks later, much to the doctors' surprise, I returned to school and resumed extra-curricular activities, including playing basketball, which was my favorite sport, and in which I excelled.

As I stood on the campus at URI, I was fully aware that I had been through something that could have derailed life as I had known it. Thankfully, this was not the case; and I was determined that this disease would not prevent me from living life to the fullest. So, armed with a large "briefcase-like" duffle bag (as opposed to the typical student backpack), I found the nearest map and then proceeded to bob and weave my way through the maze of buildings to my destination: Roosevelt Hall, home of Career Services.

Behind the Career Services reception desk sat a kind elderly woman. "Can I help you?" she asked. "Yes, you can. I'd like to speak to someone about my classes, my major, and my life plans." She smiled and said "You'll need an appointment with a counselor, but it's too early in the semester. How about three weeks from today at this time?" "Okay, I'll see you then... Thank you!"

I know many of you might be thinking, how many students seek out Career Services as a first-semester freshman? The answer is far too few. For many students, it seems to be completely overlooked until graduation is looming. I have asked myself and others over the course of several years about this phenomenon. Is there anything that can be done to set young college persons on an early path towards self awareness, self evaluation, and decision making, skills that will serve them well in their personal and professional lives? I happen to believe we can.

Bounding down the stairs from Career Services, I thought of my parents. They divorced when I was seven years old. My mother was a former schoolteacher who became a full time Mom while my two siblings (older sister and younger brother) and I were growing up. She was always there for me, whether it was urging me on in sports, giving me advice on girls, or coaching me in my school work. My relationship with my father was a bit different, almost businesslike if you will. He owned his own business, a clothing manufacturing company, and worked hard to grow the business. When it came to discussing my college options, my mother said, "Go where you will be happy," and my father agreed to pay the tuition each year, as long as I promised to work during the summer to cover all the other expenses. This understanding with my father, plus the "investment" on my part, made me take college more seriously than I otherwise might have. My grandfather, a well known speechwriter and a voracious reader, was another source of inspiration to me. I could go to him about anything: school, sports, music, and know that I'd walk away with an answer... or at least some clarity. I believe all of these relationships strongly influenced my willingness to seek out the guidance of adults who I thought could help me. Of course, I wasn't smart enough to realize this back then; but as I look back, I see the pattern developing.

The next three weeks, as I waited for my appointment with Career Services, were a flurry of activity... getting acclimated, finding my way around, figuring out my classes (what was I getting myself into with Philosophy 101?), and making new friends. One of my closest and dearest friends turned out to be someone completely unexpected.

On the scheduled day, I returned to the Career Services center for my appointment. "I'm so sorry," stated the same woman from behind the desk. "I didn't realize you were a freshman – you'll need to wait another three weeks for an appointment." I know my heart sank, and my face must have done the same. "Is this a problem?" the woman asked. "Yes, it is, I need to speak with your boss." "We don't have a boss," she replied," but I can see if the Director is here. Wait a few minutes please."

Roughly ten minutes later, a distinguished man wearing a blue oxford shirt, tie, and slacks, carrying a planner under his arm, began walking toward the students' area from the long corridor. With a firm handshake and unwavering eye contact, he introduced himself as Bill Wright-Swadel. "How can I help you, Randy?" "Mr. Swadel... [interruption – "Please call me Bill"]... I have a few questions that I need answers to." Without another word, Bill nodded and led the way to his office just down the hall. What started out as a "few questions," led to lunch... and what would become a "standing date" that took place at least once a month for the next four years. If you're paying attention, this translates into more than 48 lunches (sessions), and a great degree more mentoring/career counseling than most people get in a lifetime. Bill will always remember me asking, "Bill, why wouldn't every student want to have what I have with you?" It is close to 20 years later, and I am happy to report that Bill and I have maintained a wonderful friendship and a stimulating professional relationship.

In my role as CEO of ReadyMinds, there is an old but effective saying I like to use when addressing staff, groups, and counselors. "The only stupid question is the question that is not asked." I have no doubt that my initial conversations with Bill showed my naiveté, but he always treated me with respect and not once did I feel like I had asked a stupid question. He was instrumental in allowing me to understand and explore my entrepreneurial curiosities and plans. I worked all the way through college (more on that in a bit); and, in part because of my sessions with Bill, I had gained confidence to try things I may not have otherwise tried. The semesters rolled by and soon I was approaching graduation. It was time to take the next step. Based on many of the conversations I'd had with Bill, I knew I wouldn't be happy working for a company that didn't offer a lot of freedom and growth potential. I was hungry for experience and success. I also knew I wanted to pursue something that really interested me, something that I was passionate about, although at that time, I didn't necessarily have the wherewithal to truly understand the idea of being "passionate" about work.

The year was 1988. I mention this date only as a reminder that the Internet did not exist as it does today, and the career landscape was much different than it is now. I interviewed with Xerox, Colgate Palmolive, and IBM. All three seemed incredibly exciting to me. After a series of interviews, I received my first offer from Xerox. I could not have been happier. Yes, I would be living in Boston, which was not necessarily my first choice; but it was Xerox after all. What could be better? They had a great sales training program, the money was good, and I'd have opportunities to grow in the company. My first phone call after I got the offer was not to my family or my friends. I called Bill. He asked "What will you be doing?" I said, "Weren't you listening? Xerox. Sales. Money!" He asked again (calmly) "What will Randy Miller be doing every day for Xerox… please think about the question before you answer." I paused for what seemed like an eternity, "Hmmm, OK, I'll be selling paper, toner, and copiers… in Boston." Suddenly it didn't sound so exciting. Bill always had a way of getting to the core of an issue in a very direct and easy way. It was never confrontational or judgmental. To this day, I think this is one of the most important skills a counselor or coach can possess — the ability to ask the simplest of questions and then listen to the real answer, not just what you or the client want to hear, but the real answer. The next trick (or skill) is helping your client (mentee) hear the answer also. These "aha" moments may seem few and far between; but when they happen, it is rewarding for both the counselor and the client. Is this scenario really that different via distance? Keep in mind, I was actually getting some telecounseling from Bill; although, at that time, neither of us might have looked at the communication in those terms.

Once I heard what Bill was saying, there was simultaneously a weight lifted off my shoulders. I didn't really want to live in Boston, or sell copiers. However, there was also some uncertainty. What was I going to do? I was confident that I would find something; and with my new-found, deeper understanding of what I was looking for, I was hopeful about my prospects.

In 1987, as a junior in college, I had started working with *Campus Connection*. They published a national magazine distributed to schools all across the country. Each school had a sales representative who was responsible for getting local advertisers to place ads and coupons. This happened to be a very good fit for me. I loved people, and selling something I believed in came very natural to me. I was also enterprising, convincing the corporate office to add a Fraternity/Sorority section. This strategy turned out to be huge as I then got all the different fraternities and sororities to take out ads, too. Voilà! During my junior year, the University of Rhode Island became the largest grossing publication in the country. In my role, I met with numerous business owners, an exposure that enabled me to gain negotiation skills and helped me realize that business owners were just regular people like you and me. There was no reason to be intimidated by them. I embraced this experience and learned as much as I could.

After passing on the Xerox offer, I accepted a position as VP of Sales with *Campus Connection*. I was responsible for managing students all across the country who ran their own editions and sold all the ads, just as I had done. The environment was more entrepreneurial than that of Xerox. The President/CEO of the company was a University of Pennsylvania graduate, and the other partner, a Stanford graduate. It was a tremendous learning experience. I saw determination, "guts," late nights, deals made, deals lost, right decisions, wrong decisions, successes, failures. These experiences allowed me to train, teach, and organize others. I also gained hands-on experience working with national accounts such as AMEX and AT&T. This was my entree into the business world and to the college market. I learned how corporations targeted and spent money on this population. This experience would one day serve me well as I began to explore potential partners for ReadyMinds.

Being in this entrepreneurial environment, seeing my decisions acted on, and being involved in strategic planning and brainstorming was exhilarating, fun, and inspiring. It was here that I really began to contemplate my own future as a business owner.

The magazine was sold to another publishing company a year and a half after I started. At this point, I still opted against the corporate route, deciding instead to join my father in his clothing manufacturing business. I started in sales and worked my way up. Eventually my father and I started our own company, which I helped to run successfully for eight years, learning every aspect of the organization — sales, finance, marketing, and, oh yeah, making the coffee and working on weekends! I did well in the business, but this industry was not where my heart was. The concept of building something that I was truly interested in stayed with me. As I reflected on my experiences and on those who had influenced me in my life, the idea of what is now ReadyMinds began to take shape.

Thinking back to my time in school, I'll never forget the day I was sitting in class reflecting on a recent discussion with Bill. Whether on the phone or in person, he consistently opened doors for me; he made me think of things I had not thought of before. He helped me to view situations and decisions in a different light. I began to get ready for every session. I would anticipate Bill's questions, and I realized how my sessions with him *motivated* me to follow up and explore all that we had covered in the session. While thinking of this, I wrote down *Ready and Motivated Minds*, thinking about how everyone should be ready, motivated, and of course, have the ability to be mindful, to think in creative and new ways. After I had written this phrase down, I realized RMM were also my initials, Randy Michael Miller. Something clicked and I knew this was a beginning… of what? I just wasn't sure. This piece of paper got folded up and securely stashed in my wallet.

What transpired during my four years at URI and in my sessions and talks with Bill, as well as the start of my business career, made me realize that I had truly been given a gift—one of guidance and mentoring. In my work with Bill, I had come to know myself and also felt that I had gained an understanding of others. I felt like I wanted to dedicate my life to finding a way to share these gifts with as many people as possible. Of course at the beginning, I wasn't sure exactly how I was going to give to others what Bill had given to me.

Towards the end of the eight year period when I was working in the manufacturing business with my dad, I methodically began to build a business plan around the idea of mentoring and counseling. I began to apply the ideas and principles that I had learned during my sessions with Bill in order to build the framework. I was committed from the beginning to ensuring that the crux of this business would be the delivery of a quality counseling experience. If it didn't meet or exceed my own experiences, it wasn't worth doing. I believed it was something that had not been done before—at least on the scale I was imagining.

I resurrected that scrap of paper from my wallet, jotted down Ready & Motivated Minds as the name of my business on the business plan, and I "hit the road." I believed so strongly in my idea, I was eager to share it, not just with my peers and others in the business world, but with students. I began going around to colleges and universities: Penn State, St. John's, Rutgers, Bryant, speaking to students. I wanted to share my own real world experiences and let students know, especially freshman, that they had the ability to take control of their own futures. I encouraged them to visit the campus counselors and utilize the campus resources as a way to evaluate their options—to think about their class selections and their future career goals. It was this "passion" (I now understood exactly what this meant) to help others in their quest to find meaningful success that sparked the counseling business model. It was the thought of reaching as many people as possible that propelled this model into the "distance" space.

Why ReadyMinds?

Fast forward to 1998. I stood staring at the newly leased New York City office space, and I began to piece my own life and my career together and somehow in this palatial space, I felt I had come home. The wheel had come full circle—from assessing myself, to exploring my options, to making tough (what may have seemed illogical to others) decisions, to self-marketing. It was all coming together—I was doing something I believed in!

The ReadyMinds Distance Career Counseling Program was developed over several years by a multidisciplinary team of experts in career counseling, technology, and business development... a key to its success. ReadyMinds represents one of the first true mergers of counseling and technology. At the onset of ReadyMinds, the Internet was not the ubiquitous communication tool it is today. Technology did not factor into the original ReadyMinds model, but clearly has become an integral part of the delivery. The field of distance and cyber career counseling has evolved quickly, and yet today, overseeing this ever-changing, ever-evolving business, not a moment goes by that I don't think of that first day at URI and of my first meeting with Bill. I am hoping that in learning of my personal experiences, you'll consider your own journey and unfolding story to examine your role as a counselor, trainer, or coach.

The Evolution of the Distance Model

I believe it was common sense and intuitive insight that brought counseling, business, and technology together as one. I thought to myself that if Bill could speak to me via phone and have success, and if the Internet would allow for personal interaction between two people, why couldn't other counselors use these two powerful tools with the same successful results. Clearly, I was not the only one thinking along these lines. I became aware that the counseling field was already exploring ways to make even greater uses of technology to advance the reach and impact of counseling.

As I continued along building my business plan, I had the good fortune to meet Dr. James Malone. Jim had a long and accomplished career working with students and other counselors. He had spent 25 years as a school counselor, a counselor educator, and a private practitioner with extensive experience in career counseling. He had trained thousands of counselors in several graduate schools including a special program at the United States Military Academy at West Point. We met serendipitously through a mutual acquaintance. The rest, as they say…

Jim brought to the table his extensive career counseling and training experience, which was instrumental in building the counseling structure. Together, Jim and I began mapping out what the ReadyMinds program would look like. Keep in mind that, at this point, the basic premise was still based on a face-to-face model. I then brought in Karen Miller (no relation to me) who had a rich counseling psychology background to work alongside Jim. She was also a counselor educator and a skilled practitioner with both career and clinical counseling experience. With the three of us on board, the ReadyMinds model—a fusion of counseling and business—began going through what would be a series of transformations and refinements.

It was through my conversations with business colleagues and my networking group that the idea of technology was slowly introduced. These conversations moved my thinking away from the bricks and mortar plan and made me think about the potential of distance modalities to reach many more people than we had ever imagined.

The idea was one thing, but to build it? It took three years. In "counseling years," not that bad, but in "business years," an eternity! First and foremost, at all times, was the client experience. How would our model ensure best service to the client? As I worked with Jim and Karen, we carefully noted the value of each component we were considering. Was it user friendly—both for the counselor and for the client? Would it integrate easily with other methods? Was the format structured in such a way as to yield clear, definable results? Was it grounded in solid counseling theory and practice? If not, could it be adapted? If so, what were the best ways to accomplish this goal? What role, if any, would technology play? Would the methods we were considering even translate to an online platform? What would be involved in that translation? What role would the telephone play? How would we track results? Do we need legal assistance? What about ethical and regulatory issues? How much is this going to cost? As you can imagine, both the questions and the ideas were endless.

While addressing and researching the answers to all of these questions, the technology platform was becoming more and more exciting. Of course, it was hard to imagine at that point just how ubiquitous the Internet would be, so just as the model for ReadyMinds went through an evolutionary process, so did the role the technology would play. What was clear from the beginning was that, with the aid of technology, we would be able to reach a much broader audience than we had imagined.

As enticing as this new tool was, especially in terms of scalability, there were many considerations from both the delivery side and the recipient side. The main focus in the overall build always was the counseling and "personal interaction." The model was constructed, built, and delivered to foster "personalization," not "automation." The ReadyMinds program was built on quality, core counseling competencies, and adherence to privacy and confidentiality issues. Technology was only meant to aid and assist counselors in the exchange of information. It was always "counseling first." This mandate was true then, and remains true today.

In addition to orchestrating the creation of the ReadyMinds Distance Career Counseling Program, it was critical that we establish criteria and credentials for counselors. We took the necessary steps to secure National Certified Counselor (NCC) status for the ReadyMinds program. For counselors wishing to become part of ReadyMinds, this credential would be supplemented with the ReadyMinds Training Program, which we had developed over a period of more than three years. The end result was a new breed of counselor qualified in not only "good counseling," but also in excellent communication skills (inclusive of writing and phone deliveries), solid technology skills, and an underlying understanding of the ReadyMinds process and motivational factors.

We believed a successful counselor must be able to motivate and truly impact the client via the distance methodologies. To ensure counselor success, the ReadyMinds certification program includes substantive templates, guides, and other useful tools. Accredited counselors master the ReadyMinds process and are proficient at using technology. The ReadyMinds Counselor is armed with tools necessary to deliver quality, ethically sound distance career counseling, thus helping ReadyMinds achieve its mission—one client at a time.

The following comments come from experienced ReadyMinds Counselors who have been asked to reflect upon their training and work with ReadyMinds:

M.R., ReadyMinds Career Counselor

"Being a part of the ReadyMinds counseling team is one of the best steps I have taken for my professional development. The comprehensive training sessions prepared me to work in the 'distance counseling' arena and enhanced my career counseling skills. ReadyMinds offers it counselors a thorough, well-designed program without limiting your own personal well-developed counseling skills and practices. With the flexible counseling schedule, excellent supervision, and a great team of individuals to work with, ReadyMinds provides a solid career opportunity for committed professional counselors."

Y.D., ReadyMinds Career Counselor

"I found the ReadyMinds Training Program to be extremely thorough and well-organized. The trainers seem to have a genuine understanding of not only the detail involved in the career counseling process, but also how these details form the "big picture" of the ReadyMinds philosophy and mission statement. I am continually impressed with the level of teamwork and conscientiousness exhibited by ALL staff members. I have noticed that by having such role models, I have become a better 'distance' communicator, from the language I use in my e-mails, to the way I conceptualize each client case. In other words, by motivating the counselors, your staff is indirectly motivating ReadyMinds clients."

"Taking part in a distance program has also motivated me to keep up-to-date on information technology and how it can be used in the career counseling process. I find myself using the Internet more frequently and with greater efficiency. Above all, I find the immediate and person attention of the supervisors, administrative staff, and the Founder himself, to be inspiring, encouraging, and commendable. It is obvious that this program values education and has a genuine interest in Making It Work!"

What Needs Does a Successful Distance Program Meet?

ReadyMinds provides personalized distance career counseling to a range of clients: high school students, undergraduate and graduate students, non-traditional adult learners, alumni, displaced employees, job-seekers, the disabled, and military personnel. ReadyMinds Counselors employ a proprietary methodology and a structured program, which maximize the use of real world resources. ReadyMinds helps clients focus on their current and future career planning and provides them with concrete career development strategies to help them achieve their goals. The program differs from open-ended counseling relationships in that it is a need-based approach focusing on more immediate goals. It is structured to allow both client and counselor to move quickly towards developing a plan of action.

The ReadyMinds corporate values are: Quality, Innovation, Empowerment, Diversity, and Social Responsibility. These values drive the company and provide each of our counselors with a solid foundation in their own business practice.

Why Should Counselors Be Interested In Distance Counseling

Convenience is king in today's busy world, and the Internet has propelled us into a 24/7 workday whether we wanted it or not. We insist on immediate access to what we want. With the demands of school, work, and family, time has become a highly valued commodity. Distance counseling responds to the needs of individuals in all walks of life who are looking to advance their academic or career options in a timely and efficient way.

Here are some facts about today's world and technology:
- The trend toward increased Internet use and reliance on technology to assist the counseling process will continue to progress steadily for several reasons that include: 1) greater cost effectiveness; 2) a general increase in the use of Internet applications both inside and outside the home; and 3) continued pressure for distance learning services (Sampson, 2000).
- According to Miniwatts Marketing Group (2007), as of January 11, 2007, world Internet usage was estimated at 1,093,529,692.

The physical "constraints" of having to walk into an office, building, or a room make Distance Counseling an option for many who may never have had the opportunity or the interest to pursue a counseling relationship. This mix of convenience and availability also calls into question the probability of having enough counselors to meet the needs of every student, alumnus, distance learner, adult career changer, job-seeker, or displaced employee via face-to-face services. Hence, the overall need to extend, augment, assist, and believe it or not, simplify the process.

An unexpected "benefit" of Distance Counseling has been the "disinhibition" factor. This dynamic may be in part due to the anonymity that accompanies most forms of Distance Counseling. Clients are often more willing to open up and share in a distance encounter. This phenomenon could have been a negative had ReadyMinds not taken the time to develop a structured, well thought out, legally and privately protected means for communication. It is the counselor's job to get to know the client as quickly and in-depth as possible. Using the ReadyMinds model, clients and counselors are led through a process that is user-friendly, but not one that can be fully utilized by zapping out a 30 second e-mail to answer a question.

The response of ReadyMinds clients has met and exceeded my expectations. I am privileged to see first-hand how the ReadyMinds program positively impacts the lives of our clients – and our counselors. There is no question that Distance Counseling is still in its early stages as far as businesses go, but it has proved to be a powerful tool in helping people navigate the often volatile waters of finding the right career. I won't pretend that ReadyMinds has all the answers, but I hope that I have helped you realize the importance of history: yours, ours, and the clients'. Yes, technology has opened up doors for us that we never could have imagined; but at the end of the day, regardless of the environment (e.g., school, college, university, nonprofit, professional association, government, private counselor, or corporate practitioner), it's the people who do the work, make the connections, and build the relationships.

References

Sampson, J.P., Jr. (2000). Using the Internet to enhance testing in counseling. *Journal of Counseling and Development, 78*, 348-356.

Miniwatts Marketing Group. (2007). *Internet usage statistics: The big picture.* Retrieved March 9, 2007, from http: www.internetworldstats.com/stats.htm

NOTES

NOTES

NOTES

NOTES

NOTES

NOTES

NOTES

NOTES

NOTES

NOTES

NOTES